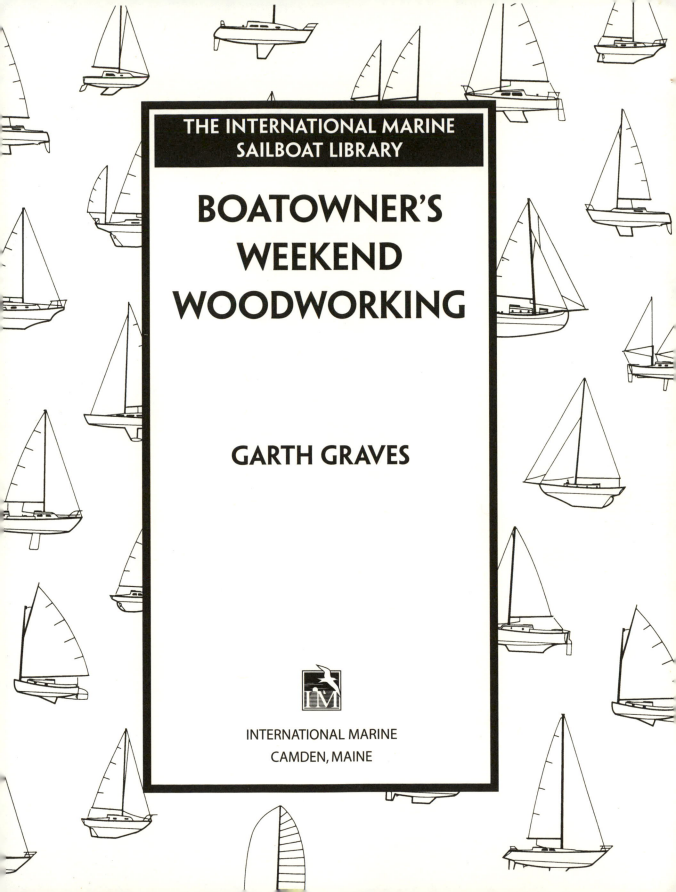

THE INTERNATIONAL MARINE SAILBOAT LIBRARY

BOATOWNER'S WEEKEND WOODWORKING

GARTH GRAVES

INTERNATIONAL MARINE
CAMDEN, MAINE

CONTENTS

INTRODUCTION

You don't need to be a shipwright, tradesman, or even a woodworker to keep the wood trim on your boat in Bristol condition. Well, almost Bristol. It is far more likely that you own a boat for the pleasure of sailing rather than for the opportunity to spend time in the ship's carpentry shop. But finding a little time to shape a piece of wood into a nice addition for your boat has its own rewards. You'll almost certainly gain a sense of accomplishment and the satisfaction of having created something beautiful or practical, or both. And there is the thing itself, an appointment tailored specifically to your boat and how you use it.

Fiberglass long ago replaced wood in boat construction, and it is quite possible to build a boat without any wood whatsoever, yet most of today's active fleet of cruising pleasure craft carry some wood. Why?

One reason is heritage: classic yacht design dictates a look that can only be achieved with wood that is finished bright. Exterior wood also softens the stark functional look of an all-fiberglass boat and adds a bit of the three Cs—class, character, and charm. Wood also gives some individuality to an otherwise "me-too" product. Finally, wood can hide joints and raw edges—a less expensive alternative to fairing and gelcoating these areas.

Today's fiberglass boats most likely incorporate more wood in the interiors than outside—they're warm and cozy below, but utilitarian and businesslike on deck. This is less about tradition and more about suitability. Fiberglass shrugs off exposure and neglect better than almost any wood. But take weather out of the equation and there are few materials as suitable as plywood for interior appointments. Plywood bulkheads don't work or groan within a flexing hull. Their lateral strength results from the alternating direction of the plies, so little change occurs in shear.

Most wooden boat components are actually an assembly of parts. Bulkheads are made from plywood that has been manufactured with a layer of teak or mahogany veneer glued to its faces. Cabinet facings are veneered plywood whose corners are concealed with solid wood molding. Doors are solid wood frames with thin plywood or overlapping slat (louvered) interior panels.

Wood is chosen by the designer and/or builder for its structural, functional, or aesthetic contribution. How well these original objectives are met varies from boat to boat. The original design may have left room for improvements. The builder may have added wood, made ill-considered (or wise) substitutions, or even omitted wooden components called for in the design. And who knows how a prior owner may have altered trim and appointments from the original design?

None of this much matters. The only issue for you is this: How well is the wood on your boat—as it is here-and-now—doing its job? Would things stay on the counter better if that fiddle rail were higher? Do the treads of the companionway ladder flex when you step on them? Are cabintop grab-rails shaky? Does the condition of the caprail detract from, rather than enhance, your boat's appearance? Do you wish you had a grate on the cockpit sole?

If your answer to any of these questions is yes, the following pages will help you rectify the problems they point out—and many others. The intent is to provide enough information for boaters of almost any skill to improve the look and function of their boats' wood in trim and appointments. If you turn into a genuine woodworker—weekend or otherwise—so much the better.

Before specific projects are presented, you will find some generic help. What are the design differences between a woodworking project for your house and one for your boat? What woods should you use and which ones should you avoid? What tools do you need and which fall in the "nice to have" category? (No woodworker—or hobbyist of any kind, for that matter—ever has *all* the tools.)

For an initial foray into woodworking, the more forgiving task of adapting ready-made accessories offers a good place to start. There is not much opportunity to foul up the installation of a length of pinrail or a piece of molding, and not much at risk if you do. These elementary projects, however, provide hands-on experience with saws, drills, and sandpaper, and introduce you to the woodworking characteristics of the wood used.

The next step is assembling the components of a kit—only slightly more demanding, but with a much greater payoff in terms of accomplishment. Chandlers offer kits for bookshelves, cockpit grates, locker doors, and a variety of other items to enhance your boat.

Dealing with your boat's existing wood is a slightly different discipline. Old wood may need more than a fresh coat of varnish. What do you do about rot in the caprail? How do you repair a toe-rail that's badly chafed by anchor chain? Is there any way to take the warp out of a locker seat? You can do a lot for your boat's wood without removing and replacing it, and that is the next step in this book. Here you will find guidance for rejuvenating, patching, and strengthening.

When the damage is beyond repair, replacement is the obvious course—but how is the old part attached and how do you remove it? Should you duplicate it or would a replacement be better? Do you use the old mounting holes or drill new ones? Removing and replacing existing woodwork is the biggest challenge for the weekend wood-worker. The task often requires ingenuity in determining how the part is attached, cunning in freeing it with minimal damage to adjacent components, creativity in improving the design, and discipline in duplicating the fit. A complicated replacement is graduate work.

In the last chapter you will find your reward for improving your woodworking skills. There you'll get the opportunity to take a block of wood, a couple of planks, or a bit of plywood, and transform the raw material into something useful and attractive to enhance your sailing experience. This is when woodwork becomes even more rewarding—when you imagine something and then go into your shop and make it. By now you may be finding that the quality of your product may be limited not by your skill, but by your tools. So maybe it is time to buy yourself a graduation present.

I hope this book sets you on your course toward greater woodworking accomplishments, confidence, skill, and enjoyment—and perhaps provide a gentle shove-off and star to steer by.

BOATOWNER'S
WEEKEND
WOODWORKING

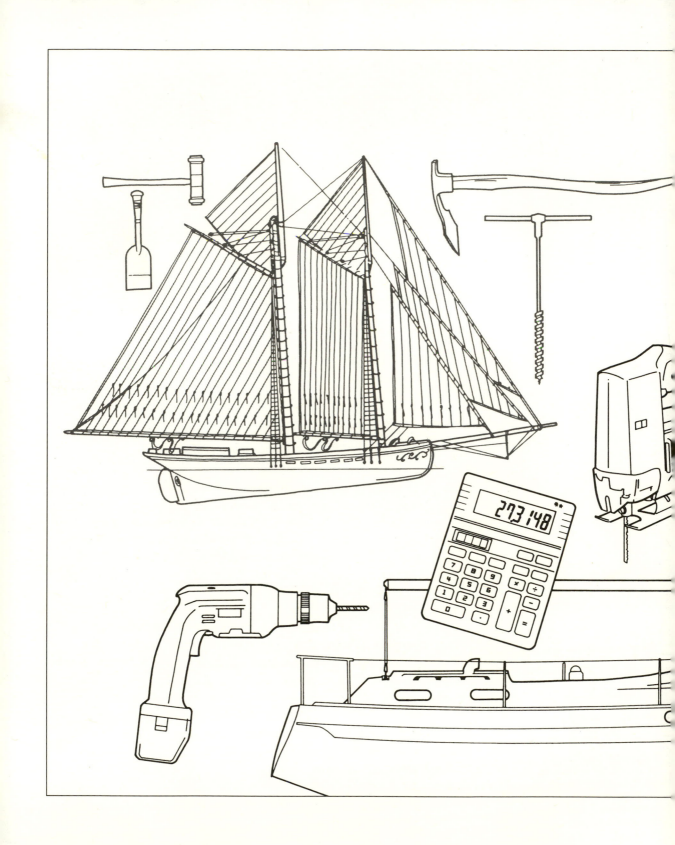

DESIGN, MATERIALS, AND TOOLS

Aesthetics, while pleasing, are secondary to the importance of function in all good design work. And in nautical design, safety is paramount. Naval architecture has evolved from a long history of people sailing and surviving. Seafarers from diverse cultures have followed these design standards and applied local interpretation, skills, and materials in building and outfitting boats to meet their needs. Your boat was designed and built with its own objectives and interpretations. Whatever you add or alter should improve on those original design objectives.

Nautical design is a study in contrasts. Joinerwork, defined as woodwork other than structural boat construction, must be strong and flexible. Some interior appointments must flex with the hull, but be sturdy enough to enclose, divide, or support. They must be rectilinear, but contoured to fit the hull and, for crew safety, without sharp edges. They must be strong yet lightweight to keep the center of balance low, and compact yet designed for the fullest use of available space.

Wood is traditional, nautical, and has a natural warmth, charm, and beauty. In a boat interior, wood contributes to a warm and friendly atmosphere. Although production boats tend to stick with traditional teak or mahogany, a custom boat might feature more exotic woods. One-off boats, those one-of-a-kind jewels, might be a mix of hard and soft woods in light and dark colors.

Design and materials come together in the process of woodworking. Using the right tools in your woodworking projects will minimize frustration and enhance the quality of the finished products. For the novice woodworker, some suggestions about specific helpful tools are given later in this chapter. If you already own a few tools, keep them handy—you'll probably find a use for them in some project described in this book.

The following pages offer one interpretation of what constitutes "nautical" for projects that you build for your boat, what woods you might want to consider for boat joinery, and what tools would help to achieve a level of craftsmanship on your woodworking projects.

THE NAUTICAL LOOK

Some shapes and forms just seem to belong on a boat. Additions that don't follow that trend can detract. Here are a few thoughts on how to follow the nautical look in the projects you build.

ROUND, ROUNDED, AND CONTOURED

Round openings are stronger and leave more superstructure intact than comparable square openings. A round disk (a portlight, for example) has uniform edge strength.

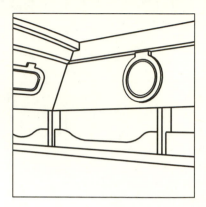

Rounded corners of doors and jambs stiffen lateral movement without the heavy framework of comparable rectangular openings.

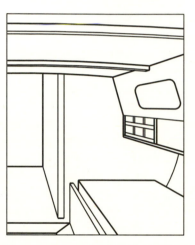

Contours are required for bulkheads, bunks, lockers, counters, and shelves to conform to the hull. Even small appointments need to snug into their space.

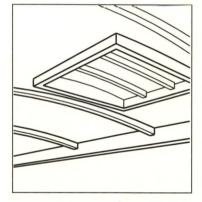

Crowned (cambered) hatches and cabintops shed water. Arched frames support greater loads for their size than straight beams.

VENTILATED OPENINGS AND SURFACES

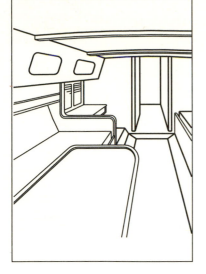

Bullnosed, beveled edges, and **rounded outside corners** help prevent crew injury.

Ceilings of generously spaced wood battens cover and finish interior hull surfaces and promote good air circulation at the same time.

Louvered panels provide good ventilation and close off the view of what is behind them. Slits, weave, and scrollwork also allow air to circulate in enclosures where mildew lurks. Louvers are a good source of ventilation in a companionway and they also shed water.

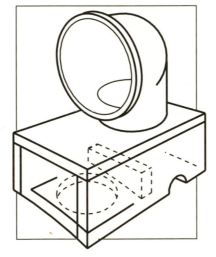

Dorade boxes (from *"Dorade,"* a 1930 Olin Stephens yawl) for cowl vents allow air flow while shunting water into a drained chamber.

RAILS

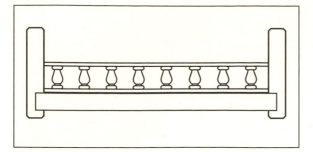

Fiddles and **pinrails** keep things in place—sometimes.

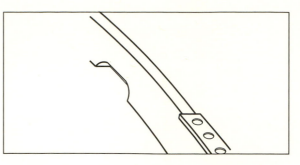

Toerails (with or without stanchions and lifelines) define the extent of your universe on the water.

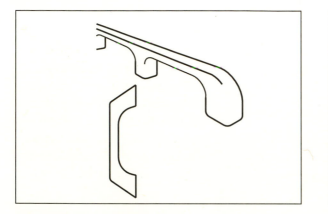

Handrails along the deckhouse and cabin trunk provide a secure grip for the sailor tending to things on deck. Handholds below deck can be overhead or cabinside grabrails, cutouts in partitions and furniture, or easily gripped posts and braces.

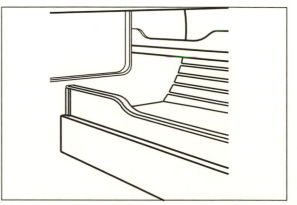

Weatherboards (also known as leeboards) keep sleeping bodies on weather bunks.

SOLES, GRATES, AND TREAD

Laminated cabin soles not only look nautical, the edge grain of the laminates resists scuffing and abrading.

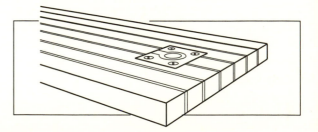

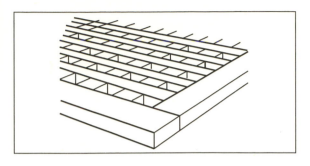

Cross-lapped grates keep feet above a wet cockpit sole, shed water between the stringers, and provide a multi-edged grip for deck shoes.

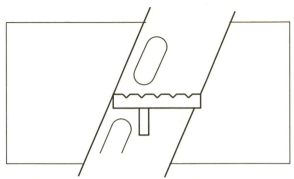

Bare wood treads provide a nonskid surface for ladder rungs and plastic or glass hatches.

BRACES AND BUILDUPS

Braces add strength with minimum additional weight. Because the strength of wood is affected by the direction of the grain, boatwrights once sought natural crooks in trees to give hanging knees in high-load areas similar strength in two directions.

Laminated members provide another way to "engineer" the strength of the part. Alternating grain direction provides more uniform strength. Because thin wood is easier to bend, lamination is used to fabricate curved pieces such as deck beams, knees, and tillers.

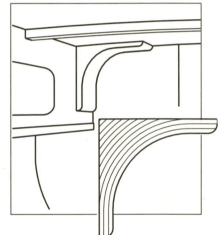

NAUTICAL DETAILS

Your woodworking results must be functional as well as harmonious. Here are just a few issues to consider.

Arcs, curves, and straight lines need to flow in transition. You can calculate tangents, but eyeballing pleasing transitions often accomplishes the same result. Use any available circular item—a coffee can, for example—as a template to draft rounded corners.

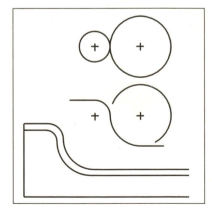

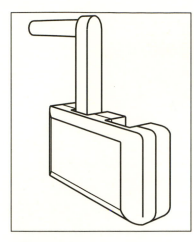

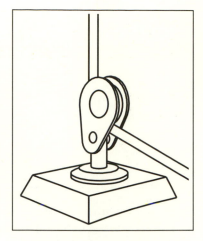

Almost all edges and corners benefit from being well rounded. Items in the cockpit—especially those near winches or cleats—must not have square corners or ledges that can catch a line. Rounded edges and corners here not only shed a sheet going by, they save a shin as well.

Doors and drawers should be designed with safety in mind. Latches must stay latched, drawers must require a lift to open, and hardware must be flush or otherwise harmless.

Pads beneath deck fittings should be nicely beveled with no toe-catching vertical surfaces jutting from the deck. A well-beveled pad can signal an early warning for an otherwise trip-prone fitting.

Ladder steps and walkways need some form of nonskid treatment. Narrow wood strips or routed grooves increase traction and direct water away from the standing surface.

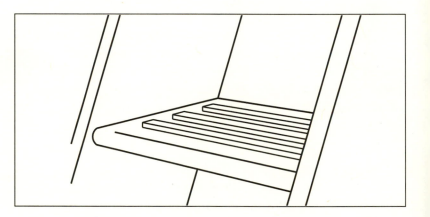

SUITABLE WOODS

Whatever modifications or additions you make should look like they belong and that they would have been done originally had the builder thought of the idea. Follow the builder's lead for material selection.

HARDWOODS

Traditional hardwoods used in marine construction, particularly teak and mahogany, are also ideal for additions and appointments. These woods exhibit homogeneous grain, resist wear, have little tendency to warp, machine well, grip fasteners, and hold a finish—all qualities that make them especially suitable for the marine environment.

If you are buying teak, old-growth lumber displays superior character and hardness. If you are concerned about the decimation of the rain forests, choose plantation-grown teak.

Mahogany is found in scores of varieties. Both Honduras (sometimes called South American) and African mahogany are superior cabinet woods. Philippine mahogany is actually lauan, and although it resembles mahogany in color and figure, it lacks the fine texture and stability of genuine mahogany.

Holly and other white woods can provide attractive accents in laminated parts.

Thomas Colvin, in his book *Steel Boat Building—From Bare Hull to Launching,* does a splendid job of describing the use of different woods with different colors and textures. Some of his observations on wood coloration include matching colors and tones with other onboard appointments. Coupling these observations with the work presented in the *Encyclopedia of Wood,* we can present a synopsis by color of a few possible hardwood species:

White and light	basswood	Reddish brown	American and rock elm
Cream and yellow	hackberry		black cherry
Reddish light	maple		butternut
	honey locust		sycamore
	red alder		sweet birch, yellow birch
	hickory		
	American beech		sweetgum
	red oak	Grayish brown	American Chestnut
Light brown	aspen	Green brown	black locust
	paper birch	Darker brown	magnolia
	cottonwood		black walnut
	white oak		

Most lumber yards carry a limited selection of hardwoods—oak and mahogany—and perhaps some teak. For a better selection you'll need to find a hardwood specialist. Some cater to the hobbyist and stock short cutoffs—hobby wood—that are too short for the professional, unless he or she happens to own a boat. Woodworkers' supply stores and catalog retailers can provide premilled wood in thinner boards for small projects.

For the project you're considering (or for one not yet thought of), you need to be on the lookout for that piece of "killer" wood. Be sure to inspect the ends of the board. If they're checked or split, there might not be enough good wood remaining for your project. If your inspired use of the board isn't going to happen right away, cut the checks and splits before they migrate further into the ends. Seal the newly cut end grain with wax, paint, shellac, or whatever is at hand.

SOFTWOODS

Some softwoods may have applications in boat woodworking projects—shelf cleats, for example, can be made from softwoods. Cedar is an excellent wood for lining a hanging locker—the aroma is heavenly. Be sure, though, to leave spaces between each piece of cedar so air can circulate. (You don't want to go to all that work and find that mildew has crept in to your locker.)

Pine lumber exhibits all the characteristics of softwoods and therefore doesn't withstand dings, bumps, or incessant moisture. Pine in plywood is light-weight and laminated between layers of glue that increase its structural properties.

With the likelihood that softwood additions will be painted, here are some species that might be used.

White	white fir
Cream	cedar, Port Orford pine (eastern and western), sugar, and ponderosa
Yellow	cedar, Alaska
Pale brown	hemlock
Light brown	cedar, white pine (southern)
Brown	cedar, western red cedar larch tamarack
Dark brown	redwood cypress

PROBLEM WOODS

Some of nature's "as grown" products are less suitable than others for boats. Red oak, for example, is notorious for open capillaries that can transmit water through its end grain like a sheaf of straws. Although not as critical in interior appointments, this is a serious problem for structural members that are potentially exposed to moisture.

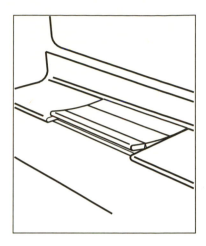

Thicker oak tends to revert to its original shape. Even white oak, a traditional boatbuilding material, exhibits this characteristic. When bent, white oak tends to possess both the strength and memory to stress glue bonds and mechanical fasteners. However, testing by the Gougeon Brothers (West System) suggests that thin strips of most any oak species, when laminated, will remain conformed to the laminated shape. Thin strips of (resawn) white oak bend nicely and can be laminated successfully, but for severely distorted forms, a denser, more homogenous, and pliable wood such as high-quality mahogany or alder, may be a safer bet.

Teak, another traditional wood for boats, presents glue-bond difficulties because of its high oil content. You can reduce this problem by taking another preparation step: wipe the surfaces that are going to be bonded with acetone or another solvent. Doing so will remove any surface oils that may prevent glue from adhering. Manufacturers of marine adhesives and sealants usually offer teak-prep products to enhance the bond.

Douglas fir (also known as Douglas spruce) is fine for plywood core, but lumber milled from this species exposes a wide range of densities and hardness at the surface that can lift and separate, especially between the softer, faster growing spring wood and the harder, more compact growth of summer wood.

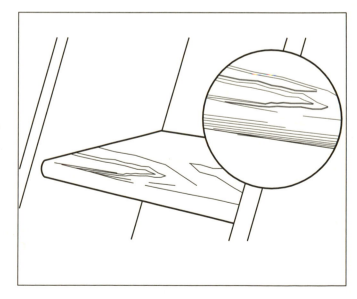

Any highly fibrous wood such as Douglas fir or Philippine mahogany, and softer woods, including pine, that are used where wear occurs, will break down far too soon under use. If you are repairing or replacing wood that will be trod upon, such as ladder treads, cockpit grates, and cabin soles, pay especially close attention to the grain and the mill cut of the wood you select.

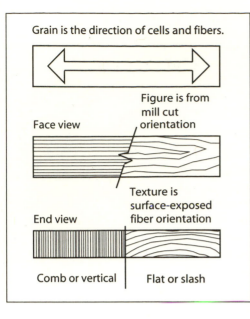

Grain is the direction of cells and fibers.

Figure is from mill cut orientation

Face view

Texture is surface-exposed fiber orientation

End view

Comb or vertical   Flat or slash

MILL CUTS

The direction in which a sawmill cuts a log and the sawing sequence affect the properties of lumber. Cuts that are tangent *to* the annual growth rings produce different coloring, figuring, hardness, and uniformity than those made *through* the rings. It is important to examine these properties when selecting wood for a specific project. In addition to color, wood exhibits other characteristics that can be useful in the selection process.

- ➤ **Grain** is the direction of the cells and fibers.
- ➤ **Figure** is the pattern produced by the grain exposed at the surfaces.
- ➤ **Texture** is the size, concentration, and packing of the cells in the end grain.

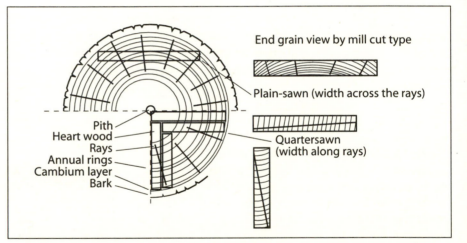

End grain view by mill cut type

Plain-sawn (width across the rays)

Pith
Heart wood
Rays
Annual rings
Cambium layer
Bark

Quartersawn (width along rays)

Cuts that are made tangent to the annual rings are, in hardwood terminology, called plain-sawn or tangential. In softwoods, these are called flat sawn or slash grain. Cuts that are perpendicular to the annual rings are called quartersawn or radial in hardwood, and edge grain or vertical grain in softwood.

Generally, plain-sawn boards have more figuring and color variation. Quartersawn boards are usually more homogeneous because density variation between spring wood and summer wood is exposed in its minimum thickness.

Quartersawn lumber is also more stable and generally holds up better than plain-sawn. One notable exception is ladder treads that are unsupported at the nose. The vertically layered grain of a quartersawn board can break down and weaken the bond between growth rings when oriented along the face of the tread.

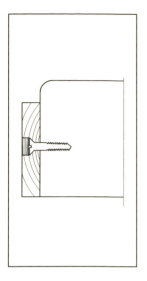

Flat-grain (plain-sawn) wood tends to warp radially toward the bark side more than quartersawn wood cut perpendicular to the growth rings. When edge-gluing flat-grain boards to make up a wide panel, alternate the direction of the rings to minimize warp across the assembly. For trim and rail pieces, orient the rings so that fasteners will counteract any tendency to cup outward.

Gussets—triangular braces—are stronger on the side that's fastened perpendicular to the bundle of fibers and weaker where fastened in the direction of the grain. Gussets cut from burls or crotches can exhibit a grain pattern providing similar strength in both directions, but most any mill cut will suffice for small projects.

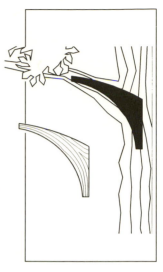

MILLED LUMBER SIZES

One-inch hardwood lumber—often called "one-by"—actually has a milled thickness of around $13/16$ inch. Short lengths are perfect for pads and placards. Longer lengths can be transformed into shelves, trim, and even grabrails.

Two-inch lumber (two-by) has a milled thickness of around $1\,3/4$ inches. The extra thickness is useful for projects like anchor or spinnaker-pole chocks.

Nominal thickness of hardwood is expressed in $1/4$s; that is, lumber designated as $4/4$ is 1-inch nominal thickness, $6/4$ is $1\,1/2$ inches, and so forth. Sizes of milled thickness for surfaced hardwoods are slightly greater than those of softwoods.

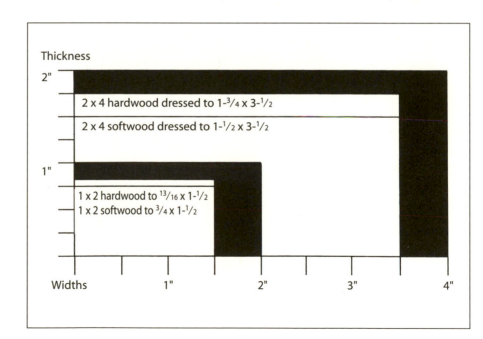

Thickness

2" — 2 x 4 hardwood dressed to 1-3/4 x 3-1/2
— 2 x 4 softwood dressed to 1-1/2 x 3-1/2

1" — 1 x 2 hardwood to 13/16 x 1-1/2
— 1 x 2 softwood to 3/4 x 1-1/2

Widths   1"   2"   3"   4"

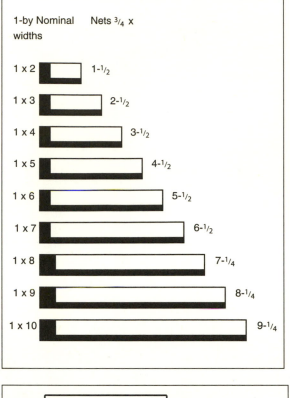

1-by Nominal widths	Nets $3/4$ x
1 x 2	1-$1/2$
1 x 3	2-$1/2$
1 x 4	3-$1/2$
1 x 5	4-$1/2$
1 x 6	5-$1/2$
1 x 7	6-$1/2$
1 x 8	7-$1/4$
1 x 9	8-$1/4$
1 x 10	9-$1/4$

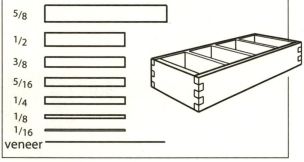

5/8
1/2
3/8
5/16
1/4
1/8
1/16
veneer

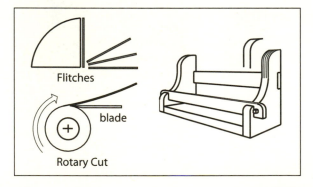

Flitches

blade

Rotary Cut

MILLED THICKNESS (INCHES)

Nominal (rough) thickness	Surfaced Hardwood	Surfaced Softwood
$1/4$	$1/8$	
$3/8$	$3/16$	
$1/2$	$5/16$	
$5/8$	$7/16$	
$3/4$	$9/16$	
1	$13/16$	$3/4$
1-$1/4$	1-$1/16$	1
1-$1/2$	1-$5/16$	1-$1/4$
1-$3/4$	1-$1/2$	1-$3/8$
2	1-$3/4$	1-$1/2$
2-$1/2$	2-$1/4$	2
3	2-$3/4$	2-$1/2$
3-$1/2$	3-$1/4$	3
4	3-$3/4$	3-$1/2$

Dressed, or surfaced, lumber widths will be about one-half inch narrower than the "advertised" nominal size, so a 1 x 2 piece of softwood really measures $3/4$ x 1$1/2$ inches. The equivalent in hardwood would be $13/16$ x 1$1/2$ inches. Take your tape measure to the wood store or, if ordering from a catalog, specify the width you want to net. Also, if you don't want to deal with rough-edged hardwood, specify that you want the lumber "S4S"— surfaced four sides.

Thin boards—$1/8$ inch up to $1/2$ inch—are typically designated by their actual thickness. These are handy for ceilings, light-duty boxes, and some rails, molding, and trim use. Very thin (resawn) stock can be laminated in a clamping jig to make a new tiller or a pre-formed arched beam.

The thinnest wood is veneer, which is available as the top surface on plywood or as a tape to conceal a plywood edge. Plywood edges can also be finished with solid trim, which additionally serves as a stiffener for thin plywood structures.

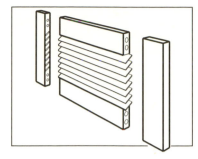

Premilled moldings, battens, railings, fiddles, turnings, pads, and blocks are available at chandleries and can be combined to make many onboard projects. Precut kits are also available for such items as bookshelves, cockpit grates, and louvered panels.

PLYWOOD

Plywood grades range from marine, exterior six-ply, exterior three-ply . . . and we can stop right there. Although waterproof marine grade may not be necessary unless the project will be submersed, you should stay away from interior and shop grades. These lesser grades, including the better interior plywood (designated ABX), are not up to the task of living on a boat. Opt for exterior (EXT) or marine. Marine EXT, an American Plywood Association designation, specifies a solid, joint-core construction with limited and filled core gaps.

Although higher grades of plywood have fewer voids and are bonded with water-resistant glue, no plywood edge should be left exposed to the marine environment. Edges need to be concealed or otherwise sealed no matter which grade of plywood is used.

Sanded plywood is marked with a two-letter grade for the face and back veneers. For example, EXT A-A is an exterior plywood with two good sides (A-A). Plywood is available with specific woods used for the surface veneers. Such veneered sheets typically have an A side and a B side, the latter being covered with designated veneer, but possibly including some patches. The A side should be a continuous, uninterrupted sequence of veneer pattern.

Premium veneered plywood is manufactured in 4 x 8 sheets, which are much too large for the projects in this book. Look for cutoffs at the lumber yard or visit your local shipwright or cabinetmaker's shop and ask if you can browse in the cutoff bin.

SELECTING WOODS

When repairing damaged wood, try to match species, color, and texture. That's easier to wish for in front of a word processor than to achieve in the lumber yard, but get as close a match as possible. Keep in mind that light woods will darken and that darker woods will

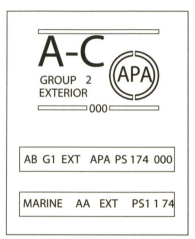

OTHER SHEET MATERIALS

Composition boards such as Melamine and MEDEX may be great for home projects, but can absorb moisture. In marine use, the constant high level of humidity, not to mention rain and spray, may soften the core. Corian is the exception. This nearly indestructible material is available in different classes and has a set of fabricating rules unto itself.

bleach lighter with exposure to sunlight. We'll talk later about bleaches and filler stains that can help you make a repair as invisible as possible.

Pay attention to grain orientation. We have already mentioned that plain-sawn boards usually show more grain variation, while quartersawn lumber is more stable and durable. In a few woods, most notably oak, quarter sawing also enhances the figure.

FASTENERS AND FINISHES

Wood is only one component of a woodworking project. You also need adhesives and perhaps mechanical fasteners for assembly and/or mounting, and a surface coating to protect the wood and enhance its beauty. Visiting your marine hardware store—with your wallet ready for quickdraw—you will find a wide selection of fittings and finishes. This is not the time to skimp if you want the most from your projects. Of course, you might not need the most expensive space-age alloy fasteners and hardware for a project that will always be protected from the weather, but even then it pays to invest in the best quality materials you can afford to ensure a long and happy life for your hard work.

HARDWARE

Items such as hinges, latches, catches, lift rings, D-rings, D-handles, and ladder hooks should be bronze or stainless steel. Stick with marine-grade hardware from reputable manufacturers and retailers. Although this doesn't guarantee that the metal is the best available, you will be less likely to encounter the inferior hardware that deteriorates rapidly in the marine environment.

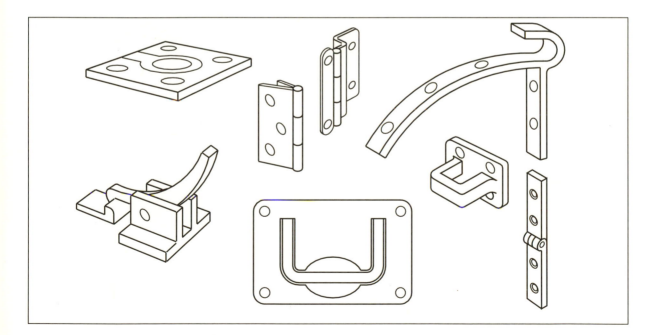

SCREWS

The illustration shows a few screw styles, how and where each should be used, the anatomy of a screw, and a table of recommended diameters for various screw sizes. Regardless of the screw style, use only marine-grade fasteners for your boat projects.

➤ Silicon bronze—Use bronze fasteners both above and below decks, usually imbedded under plugs.

➤ Stainless steel—Stainless steel screws provide a more finished look where screw heads are exposed, but may also be used under wooden plugs.

➤ Brass screws—Brass should not be used for exterior fastenings and will oxidize below decks.

➤ Galvanized screws—The rough surface of galvanized screws tears the wood fibers when inserted, thereby weakening the hold.

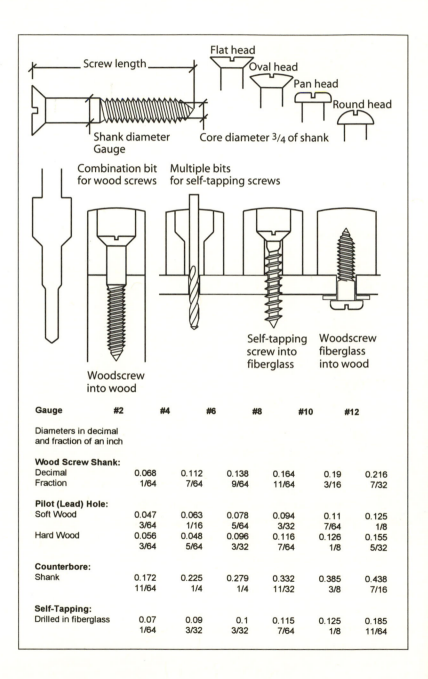

Gauge	#2	#4	#6	#8	#10	#12
Diameters in decimal and fraction of an inch						
Wood Screw Shank:						
Decimal	0.068	0.112	0.138	0.164	0.19	0.216
Fraction	1/64	7/64	9/64	11/64	3/16	7/32
Pilot (Lead) Hole:						
Soft Wood	0.047	0.063	0.078	0.094	0.11	0.125
	3/64	1/16	5/64	3/32	7/64	1/8
Hard Wood	0.056	0.048	0.096	0.116	0.126	0.155
	3/64	5/64	3/32	7/64	1/8	5/32
Counterbore:						
Shank	0.172	0.225	0.279	0.332	0.385	0.438
	11/64	1/4	1/4	11/32	3/8	7/16
Self-Tapping:						
Drilled in fiberglass	0.07	0.09	0.1	0.115	0.125	0.185
	1/64	3/32	3/32	7/64	1/8	11/64

SCREW TERMINOLOGY

Pilot hole—Also called a lead hole, a pilot hole marks the fastener location in the piece below and helps guide the drilling of larger, in-line holes to fit the screw size.

Shank diameter—The diameter of a screw, or the gauge, before cutting the threads.

Core diameter—The diameter of a screw at the thread valleys.

Gauge—The number designation for screw (shank) diameter, usually combined with screw length—e.g., $3/4$ #6, or $3/4$-6, to identify a #6 screw that is $3/4$-inch long.

Countersink—A chamfered indentation to receive the bevel of the screw head.

Counterbore—An in-line hole that allows the screw head to sit below the surface. The screw is often hidden by a wooden plug that fits into the counterbore.

Bung—A wooden plug covering an imbedded fastener.

Combination bit—A drill bit that bores the pilot hole, shank clearance hole, countersink hole, and counterbore hole in one operation. Each bit is designed for a particular screw size.

Tapered bit—A drill bit that approximately matches the shape of the screw. It usually comes with a collar stop to control depth. Tapered bits are good in softer woods but may not allow enough clearance in harder materials.

ADHESIVES

Like almost every other marine product, adhesives, or glues, are available in many varieties. Consider the following for each project: Is the project a repair job, are you replacing old or broken gear, or are you building something new? How much bonding strength is needed? How much (or how little) exposure to the elements will the project receive?

Yellow (woodworker's or carpenter's) glue is excellent for a boat's interior wood-to-wood bonding. These glues are typically aliphatic resin-based with holding strength that is far superior to white (craft) glue. Because yellow glue is thermoplastic, high heat will soften it and moisture will weaken it.

Any adhesives that you use outside must, of course, be waterproof. Two-part adhesives on the market include epoxy, Resorcinol, and Urac (the latter two mix with water or formaldehyde). All are thermosetting, catalyst-activated, and will not weaken or soften when exposed to heat or moisture.

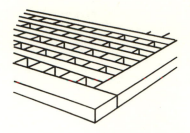

Interior (thermoplastic)		Exterior (thermosetting)	
Type	**Feature**	**Type**	**Feature**
White glues	Unsuitable	Yellow glues	Water-resistant
Yellow glues	Wood-to-wood	Resorcinol	Waterproof
Waterproof;			
Epoxy	Dissimilar materials;	Epoxy	Chemical-resistant;
	Galley items		thickens to bond
Contact cement	Thin overlay bonding		uneven surfaces

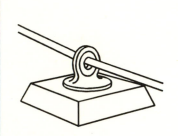

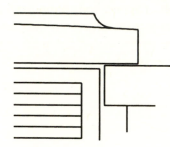

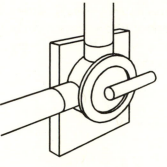

Adhesives/Sealants:

Polysulfides	**Polyurethanes**	**Silicones**
3M Marine 101	Sikaflex	GE Silicone II
Boat Life's Life Caulk	3M Marine 5200	3M Marine Grade

Uses:

Flexible:	Permanent:	Mildew resistant:
joints, seams	bedding/sealing	deters mildew
bedding deck pads		

SEALANTS

Deck-mounted items must be bedded on an appropriate sealant to prevent moisture from penetrating the deck through the mounting holes. And where the item mounts into or through wooden deck pads, the bedding also seals the wood from deck moisture. Cure times range from hours to days. After the sealant is set but before it's cured, trim the excess neatly away with a razor knife. (Masking the surrounding surfaces is always worth the extra effort.)

FINISH

A good finish begins with proper preparation. Wood from the mill can show planer marks or belt-sander tracks, or the wood fibers may have simply expanded and contracted with age. It's always necessary to sand wood when preparing it for finishing.

You might choose to paint or oil your project, but varnish is the most likely finish. Varnish is a mixture of oils and resins. More oil in the mixture produces a softer, more elastic, and slower drying varnish. More resin yields a harder and faster drying finish. Harder varnishes, particularly those incorporating urethane resins, are recommended for areas with foot traffic. The softer spar varnishes are generally better for exterior applications. Although ultraviolet blockers are a wise choice in varnishes that are subject to direct sunlight, interior surfaces get sufficient exposure to the sun to also justify UV-inhibited varnish.

80 grit for rough shaping only.

100 grit for rough smoothing.

120 grit for finish sanding raw wood.

180 grit for smoothing first coat lift.

220 grit for sanding between dried coats of varnish.

TOOLS

Shipwrights have long relied on great amounts of skill and sometimes even greater amounts of patience in plying their craft. Today's wooden boatbuilders still use yester-day's hand tools, not because of nostalgic ties to the past, but because they still work the best for their intended purpose. Even though you're not building a wooden boat, you still need some good, basic tools to create wooden accessories and make a few repairs.

WHAT YOU NEED

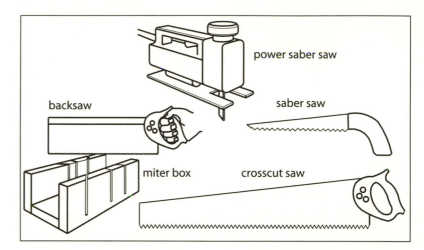

A saw is the first tool you will use on almost any woodworking project. Although handsaws can do the job, cuts are much easier and likely truer when made with electric saws. There are several types on the market, but if you are buying only one, make it a sabersaw. This versatile tool makes straight cuts, saws curves, and can make cutouts in the middle of a board. A variable-speed sabersaw and fine-toothed blade will even let you cut veneer cleanly. If you plan to do a lot of cabinet-style woodworking, consider investing in a small table saw.

A miter box is a helpful accessory for cutting true angles. A backsaw with a finer tooth pattern and rigid spine to eliminate whipsaw is nice to have but not essential for sawing true cuts.

A chisel is often the best tool for minor shaping and for making the cutout (mortise) for flush-mounted hardware. For the weekend woodworker, nearly any flat wood chisel will do. A keen edge will help your craftsmanship. A set of wood chisels ranging in widths from $1/4$ inch to 1 inch offers a good selection for all sorts of different chiseling tasks.

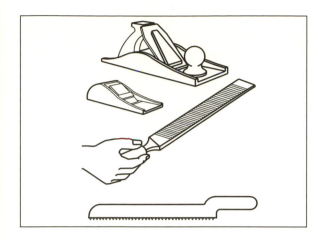

Files, rasps, and rifflers are all handy if you have them. If not, you are likely to find an inexpensive forming tool (Surform or Microplane) adequate for your rough-shaping needs. For finer shaping, a plane is the wood-worker's tool of choice. A small block plane is perhaps the most versatile; it can plane end grain, form breaks and bevels and, with a light touch, even round edges. But a long-sole bench plane is the best tool for truing and smoothing an outside surface.

An electric router is an easier-to-use, and probably less expensive, alternative to the bench plane. Not only can a router smooth-plane a straight or curved edge, it can bullnose the same edge or cut a perfect rabbet along it. A router can also cut rounded or V-groove veins, carve designs, and produce rounded, beveled, and decorative molding.

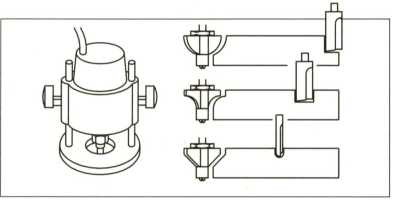

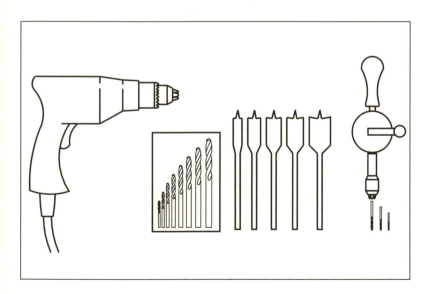

A single power drill can handle all of your drilling requirements. If you are buying a new drill, select one with a $3/8$-inch keyless chuck that is reversible and has variable speeds. Cordless drills are more expensive and less powerful, but they're particularly handy for a boat on a mooring. A small hand drill will be put to good use as well.

A set of good-quality twist drills should suffice for most drilling requirements. For drilling more than a few plugged holes, consider buying an adjustable combination bit. Large-diameter holes will require spade or Forstner bits.

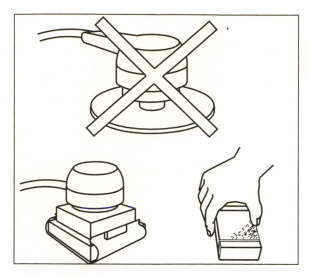

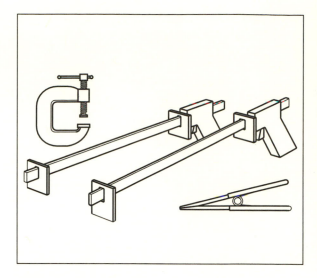

Your sanding block can be a manufactured version or simply a 1 x 2 cutoff. For heavier sanding tasks you will need a high-speed palm sander. A sanding drum to fit your power drill will be handy for dressing curves. If your woodworking plans justify the expense, a bench sander is a particularly handy shop tool—either a belt sander or a combination belt/disk/drum/spindle model. Leave your disk sander at home.

Clamps haven't been motorized or automated yet, but some new quick-grip models can perform many different holding tasks. When used in conjunction with C-clamps, spring clamps, and maybe a few pipe or bar clamps, quick-grip clamps will let you adhere to the adage, "Don't make the fastener bring the piece into position." Clamp the piece where it's supposed to go, then fasten it in place. You can never have too many clamps.

SHARPENING AND HONING

Sharp cutting edges are essential for good-quality woodwork. To keep a keen edge on your chisels and planes you must use a whetstone. Some stones come with different grits on opposite sides—coarse to form a blade edge and fine to hone that edge to the necessary sharpness.

Sharpen chisels (even new chisels need sharpening) by honing a "microbevel" at about 5° to the primary bevel. Hone the blade with a figure eight motion while applying light pressure. A little bit of oil on the stone will capture the metal grindings in a slurry and prevent them from impregnating the stone's surface. Finish sharpening by turning the chisel over and honing the flat side to remove the edge burr that will have formed. Plane irons can be sharpened in a similar manner, but any serious shaping or grinding on wide blades should be done professionally.

Protect cutting edges by keeping chisels sheathed—don't ever let them kick around in a tool box.

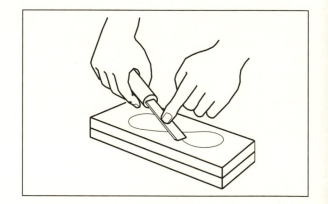

MEASUREMENT AND LAYOUT

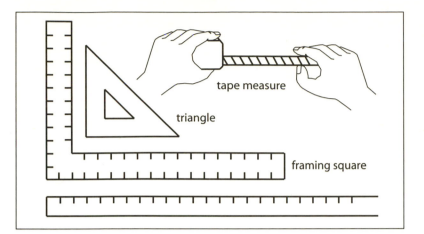

tape measure

triangle

framing square

Your navigational plotting tools can meet many of the layout requirements of your wood-working projects, but a few measuring and marking aids will prove helpful.

Straight lines. For starters, a good-quality steel tape measure is a must, as is a fairly long metal straight-edge. A carpenter's framing square is also useful; it serves as both a square and a straightedge.

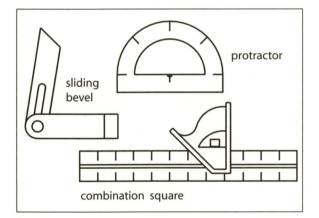

protractor

sliding bevel

combination square

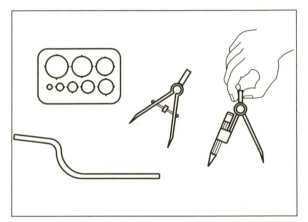

Angles. A combination square is designed to serve as both a try square (90°) and a 45° miter guide. It is also a depth and height gauge, and some contain a bubble level (which you can ignore when bobbing around at your mooring). For capturing and transferring angles other than 45° and 90°, you'll find that an adjustable sliding bevel is convenient. A protractor can also do the job.

Curves. A pencil compass is essential for drawing circles and arcs, and it can also serve as dividers. For small arcs you are likely to find a circle template easier to use. You also will find that a flexible curve is easier to use than a French curve for drawing fair curves on a pattern or board.

WOODWORKING SAFETY

Even when building only small products for your boat, an awareness, concern, and respect for safety is important. The same guidelines that apply when working with large tools and large projects apply here.

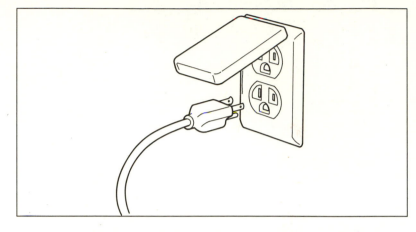

Unless your power tools are double insulated or cordless, they must be properly grounded.

Always wear protective goggles when using power tools, especially when sanding and grinding.

Earplugs or earmuff-style hearing protectors may not seem crucial for small and infrequent projects, but take it from me, decibels take their toll.

(What did he say?) Further, protecting your ears not only saves your hearing, it reduces fatigue.

You should also make it a habit to protect your lungs by wearing a dust mask when sanding or grinding. A disposable paper mask is adequate for quick sanding projects, but for longer exposure or when working in a confined space or with chemical vapors, you will need a respirator.

And speaking of vapors, be sure to follow the recommendations of the chemical manufacturers for the proper handling, storage, and disposal of these products.

KITS AND OFF-THE-SHELF PROJECTS

Let's start with a walk through your favorite chandlery or a thumb through a chandler's catalog. Most offer, or can get, ready-to-assemble wooden accessories that might be fitting additions to your boat. Maybe you've long thought a pinrail would make a shelf more useable, or that a fiddle rail along a galley countertop or navigation table would keep onions or pencils (respectively) in place. These projects are readily doable, even for the nonwoodworker.

A little more involved, but also doable, are precut kits for making your own cockpit grates, louvered doors, and panels. Chandlers also sell ready-made accessories you can install "as is," modify to fit your space and needs, or use as a starting point for building something similar but tailored especially to your boat.

Chandler offerings not made of wood might lead to woodworking projects. A clock and a barometer, for example, might look best grouped together on a varnished plaque. An inclinometer and even those ever-welcome regulation placards that adorn every boat can be dressed up with a wooden mounting plaque. Even the installation of functional gear such as vents, blocks, and fairleads often can be improved by using wooden deck pads.

Starting with precut items lets you begin with *fastening* a project (saving *fashioning* one for later). And, even if you just install an off-the-shelf accessory, the process can still acquaint you with some woodworking terms and techniques, familiarize you with the characteristics of the species of wood, and open an opportunity to consider the spatial relationships between the accessory and its surroundings.

COMMERCIAL WOOD PRODUCTS

Ready-made wooden products in pieces, modules, or whole assemblies can be purchased off-the-shelf to enhance the comfort and appearance of your boat. Some come with instructions; for others, the installation method will be obvious.

Most chandlers—national, local, and catalog outlets—carry wood products. Some, such as West Marine and Hamilton Marine (in Maine), offer a full line of teak products and accessories. Woodwork manufacturers such as H & L Marine may also publish a catalog and sell directly to boaters. Another potential source of appropriate wood products is your local RV store.

Specific items readily available in suitable woods include

➤ pinrail by the foot
➤ louver kits for vent panels and doors
➤ grate kits for cockpit, shower sole, or icebox
➤ hardware and precut teak for swim-ladder construction
➤ lots of specialty molding, including
  • inside and outside rounded corner channel for countertops and tables
  • forward and reverse rounded molding for bulkhead trim
  • corner molding designed to conceal the exposed edges of either $1/2$-inch or $3/4$-inch plywood
  • inside and outside molding for rounded door panels

Taking maximum advantage of available products, your choices are to

➤ buy and install a finished product
➤ buy a kit, assembling and installing the precut parts
➤ use the building block approach, tailoring, fitting, assembling, and installing a project made up of some or all precut parts

The cost of milled pieces is sometimes little more than you would pay for an equivalent amount of choice lumber.

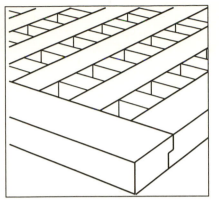

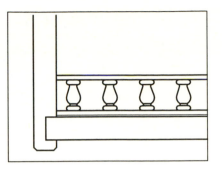

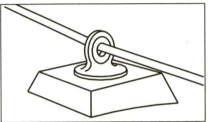

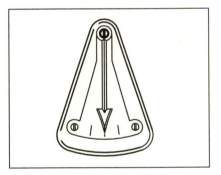

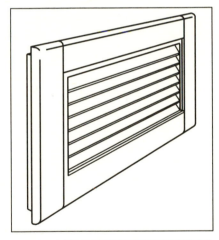

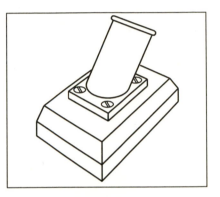

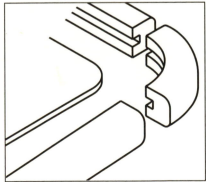

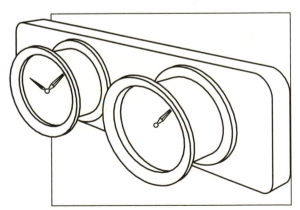

INSTALLING PINRAILS

Pinrails along the front of a shelf or along a cabinet top keep small, light items in place while underway. Fabricated pinrail is sold by the foot or in standard sections (typically 5 feet), ready to be cut to length, oiled or varnished, and installed.

MATERIALS:

Manufactured pinrail, carpenter's glue, round-head wood screws or finishing nails

TOOLS:

Backsaw, miter box, nail set

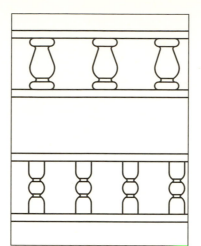

Pinrails are available in a variety of styles—from traditional to contemporary—with differing rail heights and pin spacing. Select a style that matches the task and your boat's interior.

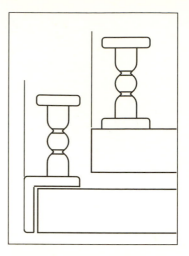

You have a choice of top-mounted (flat) or face-mounted (ell) bases. Ell-based pinrail is an easy way to finish the raw edge of a shelf.

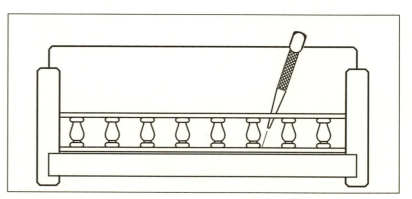

To add a rail to an existing shelf between ends or partitions, cut the rail to length, apply the finish of choice, and install. If nothing too heavy will be stowed behind the rail, you may glue it into position. Consider reinforcing the rail with small brads through the base. Hide the brads behind the pins, drive their heads beneath the surface with a nail set, and fill the holes with a putty stick.

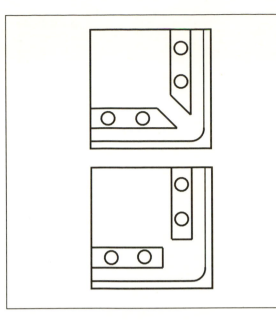

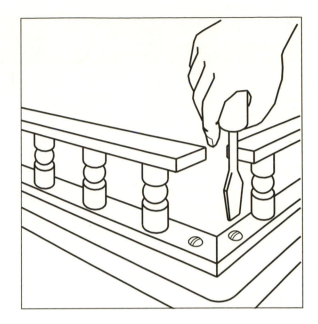

A corner can be a closed miter or have an opening for dusting away the crumbs. Another design variation is to square cut the pieces just short of the corner. Bevel the base or round it at the cutoff.

You can combine cuts by mitering the base rail and squaring off the upper rail. Shortening the top rail has the advantage of providing clearance to screw the lower rail to the shelf.

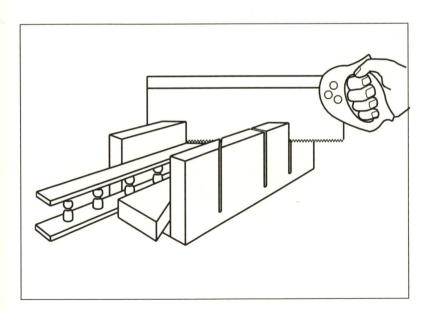

Mark miter cuts with a combination square, or for greater accuracy cut the pinrail with a backsaw and miter box.

FIDDLE RAILS AND OTHER MOLDINGS

For counters, a solid rail may be more suitable than pin-rail; for tabletops, a low-profile edge can be more practical. Both chandlers and lumber suppliers offer a wide range of wood moldings that can be used to trim existing installations or new projects. Build-it-yourself projects later in this book will make use of commercial moldings.

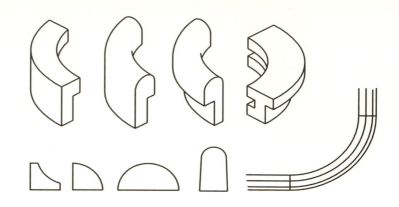

Molding is used to hide gaps and as finishing trim. Cross-section shapes include quarter-round, half-round, cove cross-sections, inside and outside corner molding, and flat battens and edge banding. Matching curved corner pieces are often available. Stock molding is offered in a variety of woods.

MATERIALS:

Molding, screws and wood plugs or wood dowels, carpenter's glue

TOOLS:

Square or miter box, saw, drill, combination bit

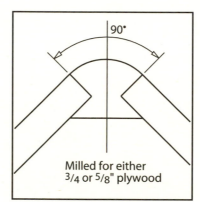

Milled for either 3/4 or 5/8" plywood

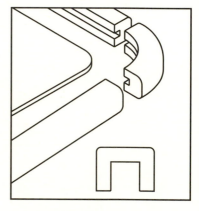

Milled corners that form a 90° angle are particularly useful for joining veneered plywood. This molding both stiffens and conceals the cut edge of the plywood. Although intended mainly for large enclosures, short lengths of this molding are also suitable for small boxes and open-tray projects.

Channel molding hides raw edges and provides additional edge thickness. It is used primarily with plywood, but it can also increase the edge thickness of solid lumber. Because channel molding offers a great amount of glue area, glue alone is adequate for its installation.

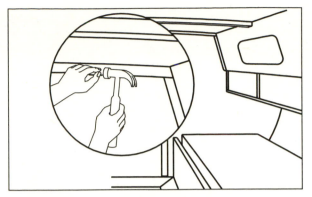

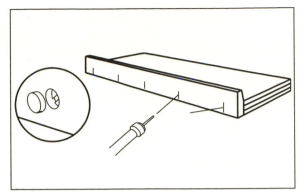

Thin moldings can be glued in place. For heavier moldings or moldings that conform to bends, supplement the adhesive with finishing nails. Sink the nail heads beneath the surface with a nail set and fill the holes with colored filler putty. Make your own putty by mixing a stiff paste of carpenter's glue and the saw and sanding dust you generate along the way. To prevent the raw wood from discoloring, fill the holes only after applying an early coat or two of the desired finish.

Fiddle rails, particularly if they might also be used as handholds, should be firmly attached with glue and screws. If the molding is thick enough, you can hide face screws beneath wooden plugs, a process that's detailed on page 87. Hold the molding in place to match-drill pilot holes through the molding and into the plywood. When installing screws (or nails, for that matter) into the edge of plywood, slightly alternate fastener angles in opposing directions to reduce the chances of their pulling out.

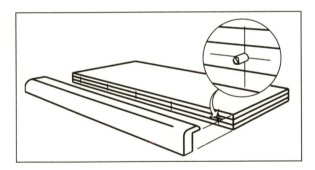

Wooden dowels can be used to fasten molding strongly to the edge of a solid or plywood shelf and, at the same time, keep the face clear. Line up dowel holes by driving small brads into the edge to be covered, then clip off the heads so about $1/16$ inch of brad shank is standing proud of the plywood edge. Align the molding and press it against the edge until the brad ends indent the molding. Extract the brads and drill the dowel holes at the matching marks.

DECORATIVE PLAQUES

MATERIALS:

³/₄-inch stock,
flathead wood
screws, wood plugs

TOOLS:

Saw, plane or router,
sander

Wood plaques and pads, either decorative or functional, can put you on the road to bigger and more challenging projects. For starters, let's fashion a mounting plaque for weather instruments and/or the ship's clock. A choice piece of premium hardwood, cut and shaped as a base, showcases these items.

Weather instruments are often sold premounted on a varnished base, but if you buy the instruments separately to fashion your own plaque, you can select a wood that is right for your boat, customize the shape of the plaque, and size it properly to fit the space it will occupy.

Most cabins can accommodate at least one, and usually two, smaller-scale instruments such as a ship's clock, barometer, thermometer, hygrometer, and/or tide clock. The whole group might be a bit much, but if you have the ambition and the room, why not?

LAYING OUT SHAPES

When you have decided where you want to install the instruments, look at the space available and the area's spatial relationships (see sidebar, page 46). The shape of the plaque should complement both the grouping of instruments and its surroundings.

A plaque should be large enough to hold the instruments but not so large that they appear lost on their backing. Decide what kind of edge treatment you want before estimating the needed width of the board. Beveling the edge reduces the mounting area, so if you plan a sizable bevel around the plaque, go oversize on the board.

Look for a piece of killer wood. An exotic species might work especially well to showcase the instruments, as well as add a bit of contrast to the woodwork below. You want a board surfaced on four sides—*S4S* in lumberyard jargon. Get the yard to cut the board square and to length (width, too, if the board is too wide) to make shaping and finishing easier. Dress the end grain with a plane or sandpaper block.

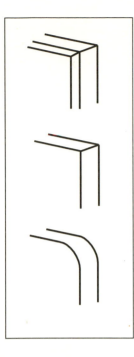

Square corners are the easy way out and, happily, can be the most complementary—perhaps with beveled or rounded edges. To cut round corners—another clean and easy design—use a sabersaw or coping saw, then sand smooth.

The traditional plaque design uses notched corners. Lay out the notches with a circle template, small round can, or drinking glass and cut the scribed arcs carefully with a sabersaw.

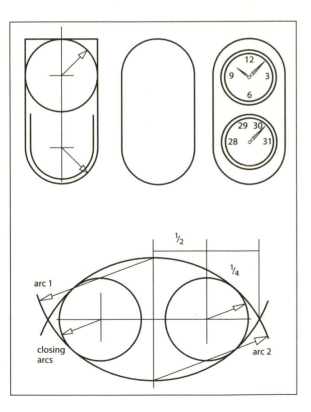

A full radius at both ends yields a more contemporary look. Draw the ends with a compass that's positioned on the centerline of the board. With the instrument to be mounted centered on the crosshairs of the radius, the penciled arc should form a constant mat around its mounting flange. Cut the arc with your sabersaw.

To create an elliptical plaque, draw centerlines at right angles and extend them to the desired width and length. Go longer on the length because the ends will be shortened when you draw the closing radii. From the shorter (width) centerline, draw an arc of the full width or more, starting at one edge and extending to the other. Draw the same arc from the opposite side. The two arcs will intersect on the length centerline. A radius the width of the plaque produces a chubby ellipse. To elongate it, enlarge the radius to 1½ or even 2 widths; doing so moves the intersecting arcs farther apart.

Divide the distance from the intersecting centerlines to the intersecting arcs in half. From each of the midpoints draw a circle tangent to the arcs.

EDGE MILLING

Plaque edges can be given a flat, even bevel by using a bench or block plane. With a well-honed blade, make progressive cuts until all four sides are even. Make the cuts with a slight slicing action—that is, while you keep the sole on the wood at the proper angle, use the width of the blade to slice the wood rather than just plowing straight into the cut. This takes a little finesse, so practice first on a piece of scrap wood.

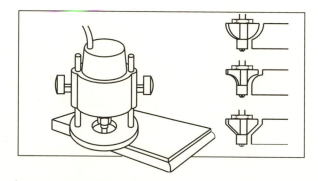

If you want to make a rounded edge, plane angled facets along the edge, then finish the edge into a radius with 120-grit sandpaper. Use progressively finer grits of sandpaper until the edge is as smooth as the surface.

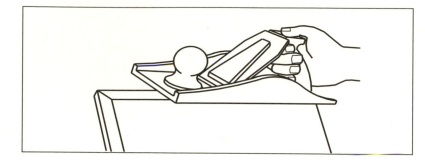

A router makes beveling and rounding a snap, and will shape an arc as easily as a straight edge. Using a shouldered router bit will prevent the cutter from wandering into the wood. With the shoulder pressed lightly against the board edge, make a shallow cut around the perimeter. Make additional passes with the cutter a little deeper each time. Make the final pass just slightly deeper than the previous one to dress the routed cut.

FINISHING

Sand the face and edge, then bevel with 220-grit sandpaper in a palm sander or wrapped around a wood block. For a varnished finish, begin with a mixture of equal-parts varnish and thinner to penetrate the wood's surface. You might also give the wood a base coat of tung oil prior to varnishing.

You can apply build-up coats as soon as the previous coat is tack-free (but before it is fully dry). Don't apply finish coats, however, until previous coats have had at least 24 hours drying time. Lightly sand between finish coats with 220-grit sandpaper to create tooth for the next application.

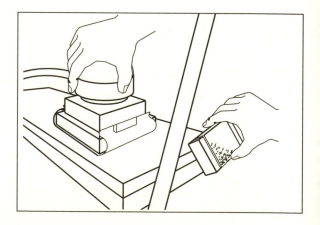

A set of weather instruments can't be hung on a hook. The plaque must be firmly attached. Mounting screws can be strategically placed so they're hidden by the mounted instruments, or you can install screws at the ends or corners and cover them with wood bungs. If you use bungs, do the final varnishing in place.

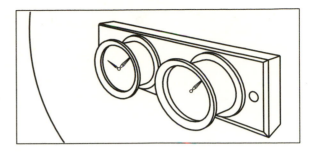

OTHER PLAQUE APPLICATIONS

The law requires that boaters post certain regulations and licenses, but there is no law against making them less obtrusive.

Design considerations and edge treatments are similar to those for an instrument-mounting plaque: the wood should create a pleasing margin around the notice or license and complement the space it will occupy.

Some regulatory statements must be presented in a size and color specified by law. For others, a bronze plaque might be a companion piece to your favorite "captain's placard" that expresses your philosophy as a warning to all who set foot aboard. Paper documents can be displayed behind a thin sheet of clear acrylic (Plexiglas) corner-screwed to the plaque. Plastic placards can be glued to the mounted plaque.

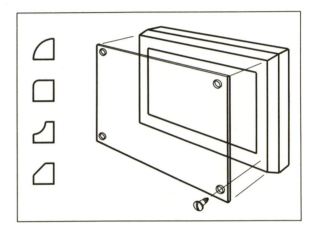

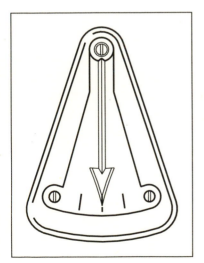

A wooden plaque makes an attractive and functional mounting base for an inclinometer. Decor items such as half-hull models or native craftwork can be also be enhanced with mounting plaques.

PROPER FIT

Because a bobbing boat doesn't stay level, measuring and squaring afloat is a bit more involved than on land. Interior structures are all oriented relative to a theoretical baseline, which you must substitute for vertical and horizontal reference planes ashore. You can approximate the baseline with a string stretched athwartships between cabin sides, deck clamps, or other points at equal heights mirrored port and starboard.

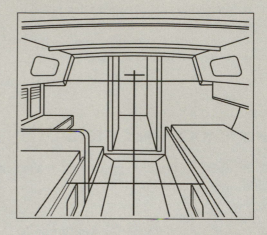

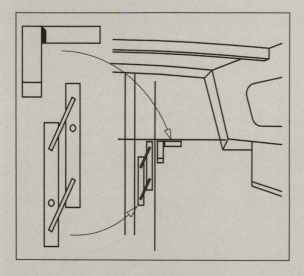

A plumb bob will give you a true vertical line, but it may not line up with the "vertical" components of your boat. An item that's oriented to true vertical will appear canted if it is not parallel to nearby planes. Forget the plumb line and use the horizontal string or the nearest vertical component as your reference. Use a square to drop a vertical line from your horizontal reference (string), or step over from a nearby vertical benchmark with the parallel rules from your navigation kit.

Getting the component square is only part of the equation. It should also be a good fit. To achieve balance relative to the surrounding appointments and structures, average the triangular shapes surrounding the area where the new project will be installed, then visualize intersecting lines from opposite corners of the resulting rectangle to get the visual center of the area. A full-size paper pattern of the addition can help with size and placement decisions.

Keep functional issues in mind. For example, instruments should be mounted so you can read them easily. Doors should open without interference. Buttons and knobs should be accessible. In fact, every project you build should be carefully designed and sized for its location.

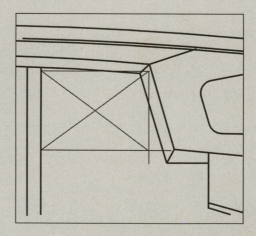

DECK PADS

Unlike decorative plaques, wooden deck pads are almost entirely functional. Whether you are adding new deck hardware or repositioning existing hardware, an appropriate deck pad can be the difference between a poor installation and a good one.

MATERIALS:

Wood (same as existing deck trim), appropriate fasteners (self-tapping screws, wood screws, or bolts), polysulfide sealant

TOOLS:

Saw, sander, drill

WHY MOUNTING PADS?

Stresses on deck hardware can be tremendous. When a piece of hardware has a small footprint, stress is concentrated on a small area of the deck. It can damage the deck and even tear the hardware free—perhaps with catastrophic consequences. A strong, oversized deck pad spreads stress over a wider area, thereby reducing point loading and greatly reducing the likelihood of deck or mounting failure.

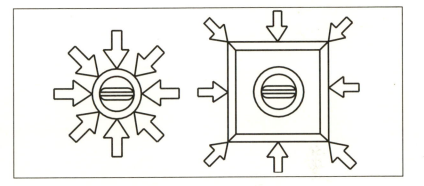

Mounting pads are also useful for matching the flat base of a hardware item to a curved or slanted deck surface. Wood pads also serve as shims to position hardware in the most advantageous position to provide improved clearance or give a line a fairer lead to reduce drag, load, and chafe.

An oversized deck pad with a generous bevel can also provide early tactile warning of mid-deck hardware that may otherwise be a tripping hazard.

DECK PAD LOCATIONS

A wood pad can be appropriate under almost any piece of hardware fastened to the deck.

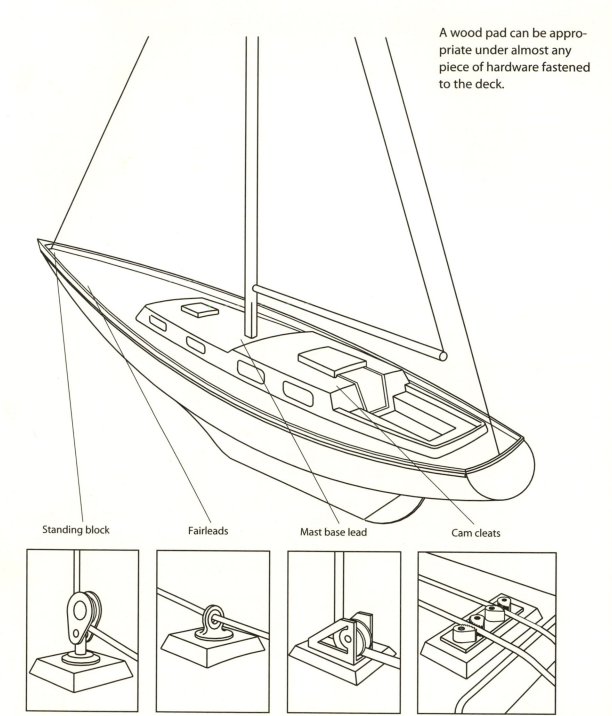

Standing block   Fairleads   Mast base lead   Cam cleats

FABRICATION

Raising or aligning hardware may determine the thickness of a deck pad. Otherwise, 1-inch-thick teak or mahogany—or whatever wood matches your boat's trim—will usually do nicely. Test the fitting on deck for height and alignment before you make a trip to the lumber yard.

The pad area should have a respectable margin around the mounting flange. For heavy-duty stresses, increase the footprint of the pad to spread the forces over a wider area.

Cut the wood to size and saw or route a chamfer on the top edges. If the deck camber is severe, or you need to align the deck fitting, rasp and sand the underside to fit its location. Finish sand and coat the pad before installing it.

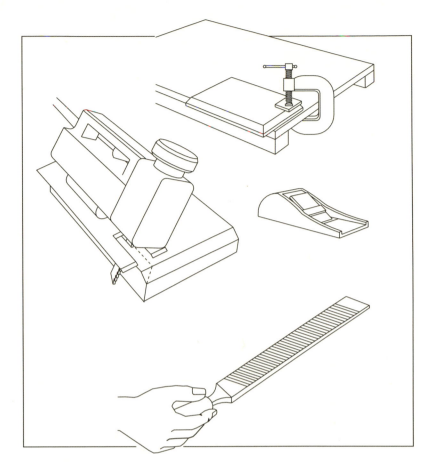

INSTALLATION

The choice of fasteners should always offer a good margin of safety. Bed the pad, the hardware, and the fasteners with polysulfide sealant.

If the hardware is subjected only to light loading, it can be attached to the pad with wood screws and the pad can be attached to the fiberglass deck with self-taping screws.

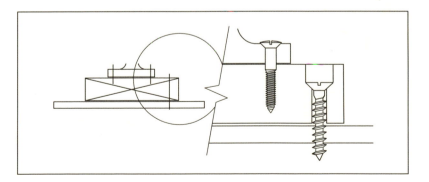

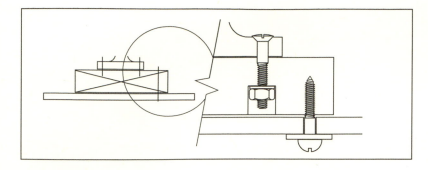

For a somewhat stronger installation, bolt the hardware to the pad, then attach the pad with wood screws driven from the underside of the deck.

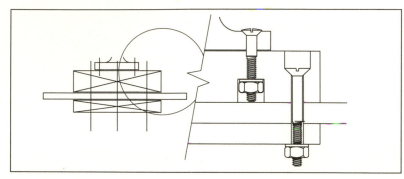

The strongest installation calls for through-bolting both the hardware and the pad. Use a strong backing plate on the underside of the deck.

OTHER USES

A deck pad can provide a flat mounting surface for a clamshell, cowl or mushroom vent, lift a bow roller over the toerail, raise a fuel fill above a wet deck, or house the socket of a navigational light. And in case you need something else to varnish, a wood deck pad might set off a chrome or bronze ensign base a bit more elegantly.

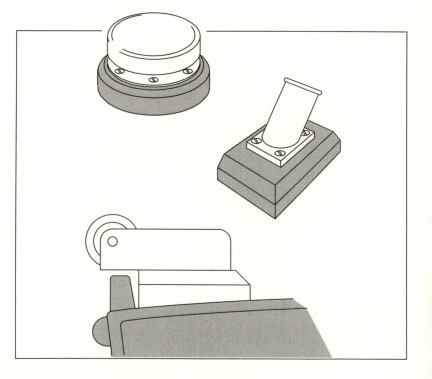

MINIWORK PLATFORM

This miniplatform provides a work area you can use for clamping, gluing, and generally banging around on. It is especially useful if you are without a bang-around workspace.

Start with sheet of ¾-inch shop-grade plywood approximately 2 x 3 feet. This will be large enough for most small projects yet small enough to store. Flank the two long outside edges with two full-length 2 x 2s, glued and screwed. Cut two or three additional lengths of 2 x 2 as auxiliary stop blocks or supports beneath the platform.

You'll put both sides to good use. Resting the platform on the 2 x 2s allows clearance below for clamping your work to the top surface. Slip a couple of the other 2 x 2s underneath to support the middle of the platform for pounding and drilling. Flip the platform over and the fastened 2 x 2s serve as fixed stop blocks to clamp against while gluing. The other side of the gluing clamp is one of the loose 2 x 2s held in tight by a single bar clamp or by a pair of wedges driven between it and the other fixed side.

If you need to dress an edge of a small board, clamp it to the work surface. For special requirements, nail stop blocks where needed, or drill a hole in the center of the platform to insert a C-clamp. While you're drilling holes, add a row for bench dogs—dowel pegs that can be inserted as a braces for various size projects. Bench dogs and midboard clamp holes add versatility, but don't get carried away and weaken the plywood.

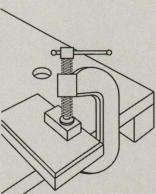
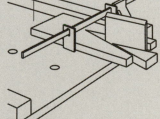
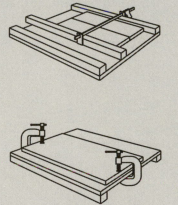
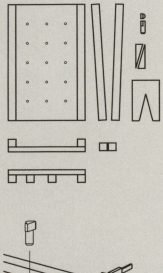

TEAK COCKPIT GRATE

A cockpit grate, besides being an attractive addition to virtually any boat, has the practical benefits of keeping feet dry(er), allowing plenty of air flow, and providing a good gripping surface for deck shoes. Cross-lapped grates are equally useful in showers, ice boxes, and as trivets.

MATERIALS:

Precut teak, wood screws, epoxy

TOOLS:

Saw, sander, drill

If you're going to assemble a cockpit grate from prenotched stringers and premilled frame pieces, all you have to do is cut to fit and assemble—definitely in the weekend project category.

Two grid options are possible: You can use matched stringers in both directions so that one notch fits into the other to form a cross half-lap joint. Or, you can use the notched stringers for the lower pieces only, with thinner cross-stringers on top that fit the depth of the notches. This method, called full-lap, may not look as substantial but it is purportedly as strong as the half-lap version and has the advantage of allowing water to flow freely beneath the grate.

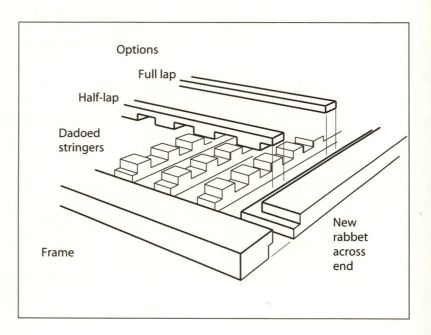

Options

Full lap

Half-lap

Dadoed
stringers

Frame

New
rabbet
across
end

DESIGNING THE GRATE

Well before your planned "assembly weekend," locate your kit source and get the specifications of the milled pieces. Take special note of the width and thickness of the stringer pieces and the width, depth, and spacing of the notches. The notch will be a tad wider than the stringer width to receive the cross stringer.

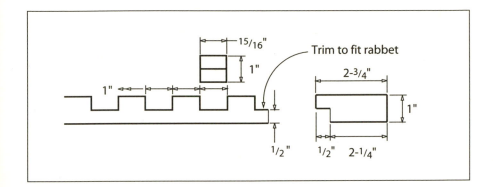

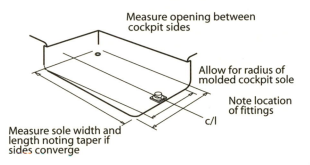

Measure the width, length, and taper of the cockpit sole. Note the location of scuppers and any other features or interruptions that will need to be avoided or relieved. You want to design your grate to

- rest firmly between cockpit sides
- allow for any radii between the cockpit sides and sole
- avoid or divide around any protrusion
- be readily removable

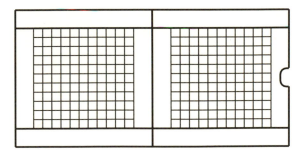

To prevent a large cockpit grate from becoming cumbersome, building it in two (or more) sections can be a practical choice. Multiple sections are almost always required with a kit-built grate because the milled components are sold in standard lengths—typically 4 feet. A sectioned grate is also indicated when there is an obstruction in the sole, such as a mizzenmast or a binnacle. Flank the obstruction between butted frames relieved with matching cutouts.

Try to design the grate sections as close to square as possible. Grates that are either too long or too short in proportion to their width may appear chopped up.

If the cockpit is wider at one end than the other, plan to cut this taper along the outside frame pieces. Doing so is easier than cutting each stringer in progressive lengths and putting an angle on each end to fit converging frames.

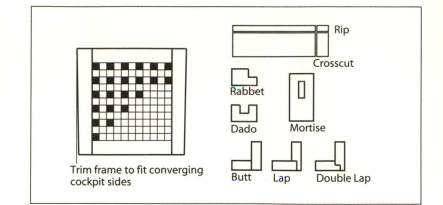

Trim frame to fit converging cockpit sides

Rip
Crosscut
Rabbet
Dado
Mortise
Butt
Lap
Double Lap

USEFUL TERMS

Rip—To cut along the length of the board, usually aligned with the grain.

Crosscut—To cut a board across the grain, usually the width of the board.

Rabbet—A two-sided step cut along the edge or end of a board.

Dado—A three-sided groove.

Butt joint—The weakest joint; two pieces fastened together with one surface of one abutting one surface of the other.

Lap Joint—Two pieces joined with some overlap. To avoid double thickness, both pieces may be rabbeted or dadoed to half thickness, resulting in a half-lap joint.

Mortise—A four- or five-sided groove.

CALCULATING MATERIALS

After you have worked out the dimensions of the finished grate, you can work up your materials list. This is where you need to know the dimensions of the materials you will be using. For purposes of illustration, let's use the actual dimensions of the grating components currently sold by West Marine. (H & L Marine's unassembled grating is also an option, but sizes differ.) Stringers are 1-inch square stock—actually, they're $^{15}/_{16}$ so they fit into the 1-inch notches. Flat stringers are the same width but half the thickness—equal to the depth of the dado in the notched stringers. Frame pieces are $2^3/_4$ inches wide and 1-inch thick.

West Marine also sells $^1/_2$-inch stringers appropriate for ice boxes and shelves. The framing for this lighter-weight grating is $1^3/_4$ inches wide.

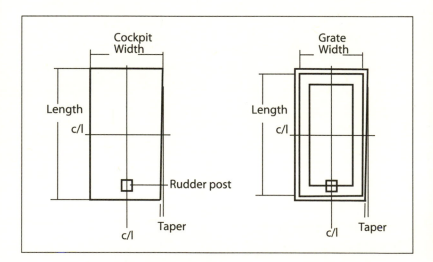

Cockpit Width
Grate Width
Length
c/l
c/l
Rudder post
Taper
Length
c/l
c/l
Taper

Again, for illustration purposes, let's assume we're working with a cockpit sole that's 81 inches long (a fair-sized boat) with a maximum width of 27 inches. Allowing $1/2$-inch clearance all around the grate, that gives us an outside frame dimension of 80 inches by 26 inches. But since the commercial stringer length is 4 feet, we are going to construct the grate in two sections, each 40 inches by 26 inches.

We can ignore taper at this point—as long as it is modest—because we are going to trim the outside frame of the finished grate.

To calculate the stringer lengths, we need the inside dimensions of the frame. Given $2^3/4$-inch-wide frame pieces, we can subtract $5^1/2$ inches ($2^3/4$ x 2) from the outside frame. For our 40-inch by 26-inch grates, this gives us a grid dimension of $34^1/2$ by $20^1/2$. As you will see shortly, this project is greatly simplified if the grid dimensions are *exactly* an odd number of stringer widths. We can accomplish this by trimming the frame width—$1/4$ inch on all sides in this case—to yield a grid dimension of 35 by 21. Visually, the frame should be wider than the stringers. Avoid trimming the frame width to less than twice the stringer width.

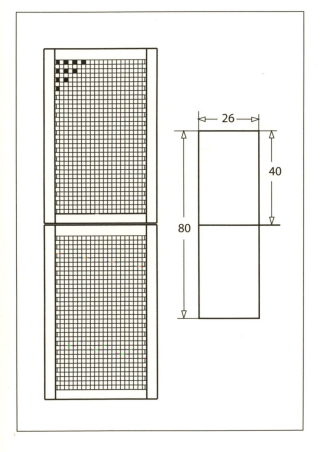

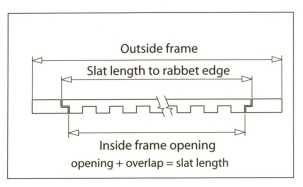

Grid and stringer dimensions are not the same. Because the stringers overlap the frame (in this example, $1/2$ inch on each end), we need to add 1 inch to the grid dimensions to get stringer lengths. We need one stringer for every 2 inches of grid width or length, so for our 35 by 21 grid we need eleven 36-inch stringers and seventeen 22-inch stringers. Fortunately, we can get two of the shorter stringers from a 48-inch piece of stock, so building both grates will require 39 stringer pieces and 8 lengths of frame material.

Caution: Don't rush headlong into this project without first calculating costs. Materials for the sample grate described here would total more than $1,000 for the heaviest, half-lap model. There is hope. Read on.

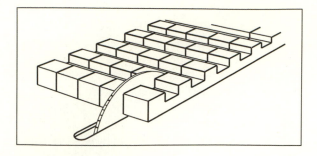

You might find it less costly to have a local wood planing mill cut the stringers. Or, if you have access to a table saw you might fabricate the pieces yourself from lumberyard stock. No matter who does the cutting, consistent width, depth, and spacing of the notches is critical. Individual stringers can be ripped to width before cutting the dadoes or, as shown here, a wide board can be notched to the half depth, then ripped to the precise stringer width that will fit into the notches.

ASSEMBLY

Frame material in this example comes premilled with a $\frac{1}{2}$-inch rabbet along the inside edge. Cut athwartship frame members 1 inch longer than the dimension between the inside edges of the frame. Use a router to put a $\frac{1}{2}$-inch rabbet (as shown) on each end of the athwartship pieces (matching the existing rabbet). When the frame is assembled, the rabbets will face up on the side pieces and down on those that run athwartships.

The earlier mention of designing for an odd number of stringers should result in the same hole openings (preferred) or solid stringers (okay, too) next to the frame opening. Whichever pattern you design should mirror the opposite frame.

New rabbet across end

Rabbet

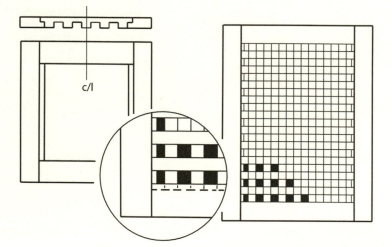

c/l

It is time to figure out the *gozintas* (what piece gozinta what other piece). You want to end up with a row of grate openings against the inside edges of the frame all around. If you adjusted the grid size to an odd multiple of stringer widths when you cut the stringers to length, the half dado remaining at each end becomes, with a good deal of luck, a perfect rabbet for fitting the stringer into the frame.

The key here is to cut the overall length (beyond the inside opening to the rabbeted shoulder of the frame) while keeping the dadoes aligned to fit the cross-stringers. Dry fit the center crossmember and measure to both ends. Notch (rabbet) the stringer ends to fit onto (in one direction) or under (crosswise members) the frame.

If you are using the flat, rather than notched, strips for the top stringers, these must rest atop the upward-facing dadoed frames.

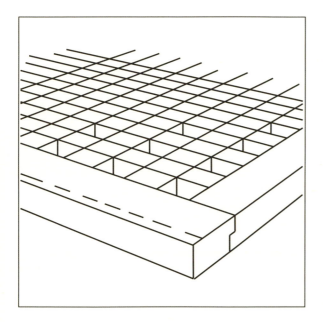

Dry fit cross-lapped stringers and frames to check for fit and size. Trim and dress the outside edge of the frame.

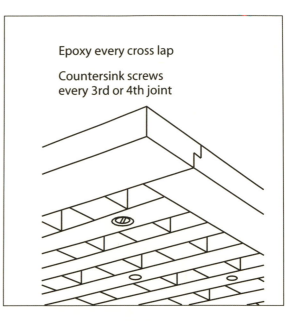

Epoxy every cross lap

Countersink screws every 3rd or 4th joint

Reassemble the grate, gluing every joint with slightly thickened epoxy. Fasten every third or fourth intersection with 3/4-inch #8 bronze flathead screws countersunk flush or slightly indented.

Because cockpit grates are constantly exposed to the weather, the teak may be left to gray naturally or given a coat of teak oil.

SWIM LADDER

A wooden swim ladder kit can be purchased complete with cut wooden parts, which gets you on (and in) the water sooner, or you can buy the hardware only to have the pleasure of doing the woodwork yourself. Ladder hardware is available new in both cast bronze and plated steel. If you want to save a few dollars, it often doesn't take much searching to find an old ladder with sound hardware.

MATERIALS:

1 x 8 teak or mahogany, bronze or plated steel ladder hardware, hanger straps, wood screws, epoxy

TOOLS:

Sabersaw, sander, drill

Although a swim ladder can be made of most any hardwood, teak is the wood of choice if it will be stowed on deck. Select solid lumber that's wide enough to allow for an appropriate standoff at the bottom of the ladder and long enough to reach just shy of the waterline (in the folded position). Determine the configuration of the near-hull edge.

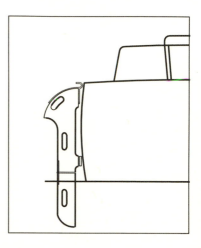

Position the ladder hook hardware and trace its arc onto the board. Lay out a handhold that follows the contour of the ladder-hook arc and perhaps a second one lower between rungs. Starting from the bottom, draw a line that splits the board in half then merges into a nice arc back to the front face. This will be the fold-down extension.

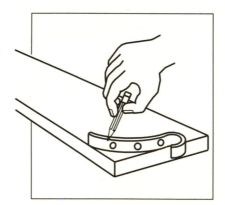

. . . and handhold

Cut along the marked lines with a sabersaw.

Lay out the rung spacing— they should be equally spaced when the ladder is in the extended position and aligned when the ladder is folded.

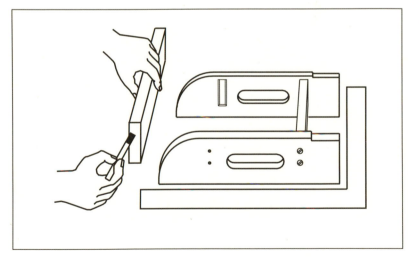

Cut the ladder rungs to appropriate lengths and widths and rout the front and back edges. Rout and/or chisel mortises in the side pieces to receive the ends of the rungs.

Round the edges of the side pieces except where the hardware will attach.

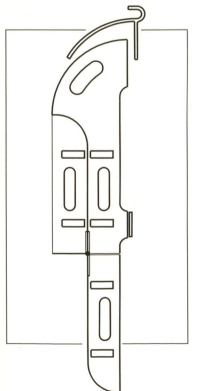

Install the rungs into the mortised sockets with epoxy glue and screws, taking care to keep the assembly square.

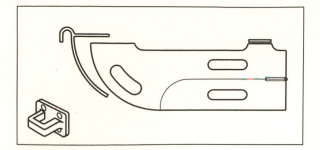

Install the hardware. If you are using a strap hinge (rather than a side-mounted scissor hinge), cut mortises or rabbets in the leading edge (when extended) to let the hinge in flush. This lets the two halves fit together properly when the extension is folded.

The swim ladder hangs from eyeplates installed on the hull. When it is not on use, special chocks can provide convenient and secure stowage. Chapter 5 contains some deck chock ideas.

ROPE LADDER

An alternative to a solid wood ladder is one constructed of rope with wood rungs. A rope ladder—also called a Jacob's ladder—is not as stable as its rigid cousin, but it stows more easily.

MATERIALS:

1 x 6 teak or mahogany,
³/₈-inch rope

TOOLS:

Saw, sander, drill

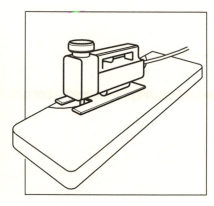

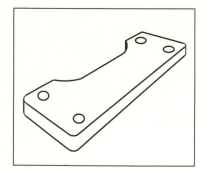

Your feet cannot extend beyond the back of the rungs of a rope ladder because your weight pushes the rungs (and your toes) against the hull. Therefore, the rungs on such a ladder need to be wide—at least 5 inches. Cut them about 18 inches long. A small rubber bumper—like the kind that's used on cabinet doors and toilet seats to keep them from banging against their mates—along the backside of each rung will prevent it from marring the hull. Another option is to epoxy some narrow extruded rubrail shapes to the rungs.

Drill holes in each corner of the ladder rung. The holes should be slightly larger than the ³/₈- or ¹/₂-inch line you use. Countersink the holes to aid the threading of the rope and to prevent chafing.

Route a nonskid pattern into the top surface of each rung.

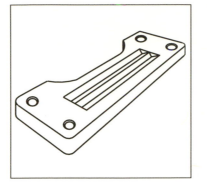

Wooden hooks may be substituted for the whipped loop. Choose either braided or twisted Dacron line. Stay away from polypropylene rope because some tight knotting is in order. Instead of whipping (or simply tying the four strands in an overhand knot, get out your favorite book of knots and splice the ladder rope into a loop.

LOUVERED PANEL

Adding to or improving ventilation in lockers is a valuable project for most boats, and louvered panels are perhaps the most elegant way to allow mildew-defeating airflow into closed spaces. Installing a louvered panel in a companionway dropboard provides additional and usually much-needed cabin ventilation when a boat is closed up.

MATERIALS:

Prefabricated rails, stiles, and slats, wood screws, carpenter's glue

TOOLS:

Saw, sander, drill

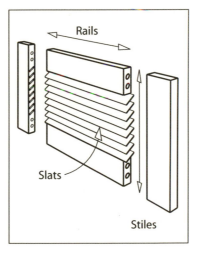

Rails

Slats

Stiles

The vertical members of any frame-and-panel assembly are called *stiles*. In the case of louvered panels, the slotted stiles are not reversible, so you will need both left- and right-hand stiles. *Rails* are the horizontal frame pieces between the stiles; the thin strips that form the actual louvers are *slats*.

DESIGNING FOR ECONOMY

Your chandler is likely to sell teak stiles, rails, and slats in 4-foot lengths, so some preplanning is needed to minimize waste—and cost. For example, if you cut a pair of 4-foot stiles in half and cut a single length of rail into four $11^1/2$-inch sections, you can make two frames 24 inches high by about $15^1/2$ inches wide (length of the rail *plus* the width of the stiles). Cutting the rail $11^1/2$ inches long lets 12-inch slats extend into the slots in the stiles, so you get four slats from each piece of 4-foot stock. Cutting the rails to 12 inches would save 2 inches of rail scrap but result in $10^1/2$ inches of waste in every 4-foot slat.

Because the edge-to-edge distance between installed louvers is typically about 1-inch, the number of running inches of slat required is approximately the same as the area of the panel in square inches. In this example, the panel dimensions are about 20 inches (24 less twice the rail width) by 12 inches ($15^1/2$ less twice the stile width, plus the slot depths). The panel area is 240 square inches (12 x 20), so we need the same number of linear inches of slat stock. Dividing 240 inches by 48 (the length of the slat stock) yields five 4-foot lengths of slat per panel, or a total of 10 slats for the two panels— with virtually no waste.

Although it isn't always possible to use the materials so efficiently, small adjustments, where necessary, can have a significant impact on cost.

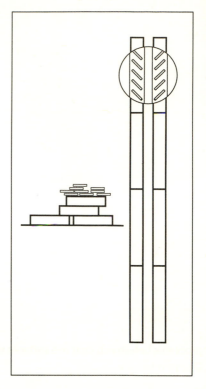

Fixed louvers are usually set at 45 degrees with enough overlap to hide the contents (or activity) behind. Slat edges may be square, rounded, or bullnosed into a half-round leading edge. Reshape them as necessary to match new louvers to similar appointments already on your boat. Sand the ends of the cut louvers for an easy fit into the milled slots.

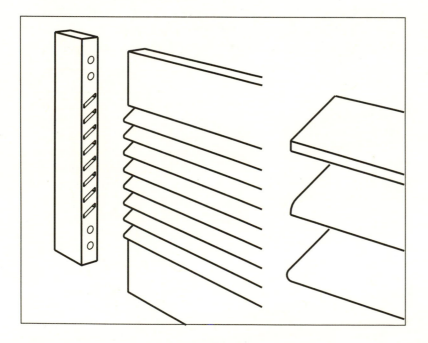

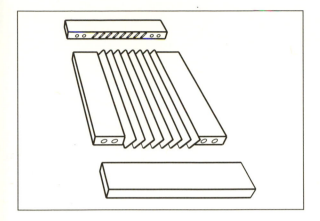

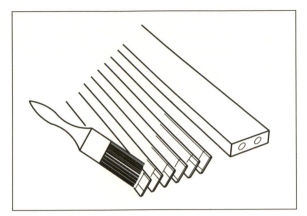

For maximum strength, use dowels to join the rails and stiles. Drive two brads into the stile near each end, centered in the edge and between mortised slots (for the slats). Clip off the nail heads, then position the stile and rail inside a carpenter's square and press the two pieces together to mark the rail. Remove the brads and drill the dowel holes ($\frac{1}{4}$ or $\frac{3}{8}$ inch), using the brad indentions as pilots. Cut the dowels to length and dry fit all the components to discover any alignment problems before you coat the surfaces with glue. Disassemble.

Applying the first coat of oil or varnish before assembly will make it easier to clean away glue that might otherwise stain the exposed surfaces. Keep the finish away from surfaces to be glued. Slat ends, for example, should be masked just shy of the depth they will let into the stiles.

After the first coat of finish has dried, apply glue sparingly in one of the stiles and in the dowel holes and mating surfaces of top and bottom rails. You can use carpenter's glue for an interior panel, but any panel that might get wet should be assembled with epoxy. Insert the dowels and, using a carpenter's square to keep the assembly square, press the end of the rails tightly against the side of the stile and clamp.

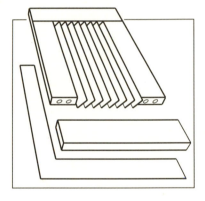

Continue gluing before this three-piece assembly has thoroughly set, being careful to keep it square. Apply a small amount of glue in the slots and on the slat ends and fit all the slats into the assembled stile. Working quickly now, apply glue into the dowel holes and slat slots, onto the slat ends, and on the mating surfaces between the rails and the remaining stile. Fit the stile onto the dowels and slats, and clamp. Check again for square, then allow the glue to dry.

If a panel seems too wide for the slat thickness, now is the time to glue spacer blocks inside and behind the slats to align and stiffen the louvers. Easier than assembling louvered panels from premilled kits, you can purchase them preassembled in a number of off-the-shelf sizes. A manufactured louvered panel typically has a rounded edge with a $\frac{1}{2}$-inch rabbet cut into the backside perimeter. These panels fit an opening 1 inch smaller than their overall dimensions.

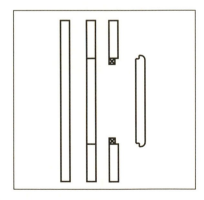

Giving a louvered panel a backside rabbet avoids most fit problems. Use a sabersaw to cut the hole slightly larger than the rabbet-to-rabbet dimensions. Insert the panel into the cutout with the rabbeted lip resting against the face surface, then cut a frame of flat molding to hold the panel in place and hide the joint on the backside. The corners of this inside frame can be mitered or butt joined, depending on your ambition. Screws through the inside frame into the rails and stile of the panel will hold it snugly in the opening.

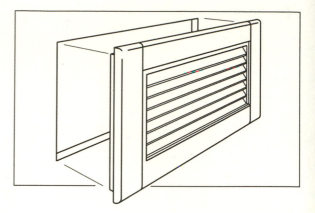

LOUVERED DOORS

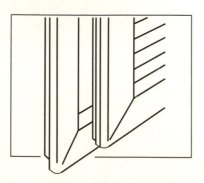

Like louvered panels, preassembled louvered cabinet doors are available in various "standard" sizes. Typically, both the frame and the door are rabbeted, so the frame stands about 3/8 inch above the cabinet face and the door stands an additional 3/8 inch above the frame.

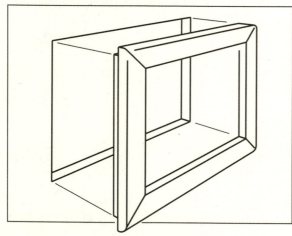

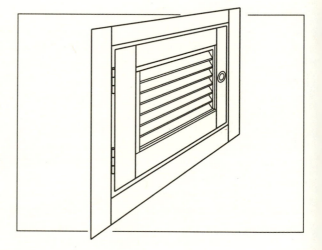

Install the door frame just like a louvered panel by clamping it against the cabinet surface with an interior frame. Gluing the frame into the opening makes the assembly more rigid.

If you want the frame, and perhaps the door, flush with the face of the cabinet, cut away the rabbeted flange. Making a flush installation look professional requires great care in getting the cutout exactly the right size and mating all abutting edges.

HINGES AND LATCHES

A rabbeted lip on a cabinet door requires using offset hinges to wrap around the rabbet. If the door is flush with the frame, a simple butt hinge will serve. Butt hinges need to be mortised into the door and the frame to keep the perimeter gap minimal and uniform.

Strap hinges are another choice if you don't object to their face mounting. At the opposite end of the spectrum are various types of concealed and semi-concealed hinges that show only minimally or not at all when the cabinet is closed.

DOUBLE-HUNG DOORS

When two doors meet in the center of an opening, they are known as double-hung. To minimize the gap between the two and still let each swing open or closed without interfering with the other, plane a slight bevel toward the back of the center stiles.

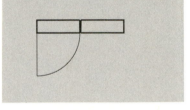

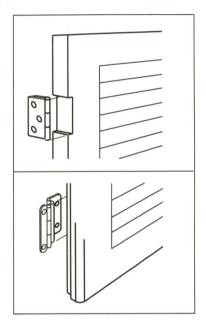

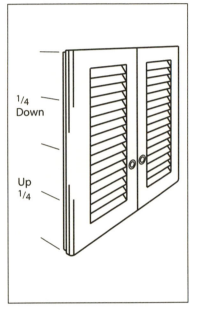

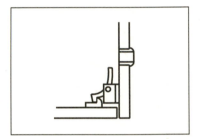

Visually divide the door height into quarters and keep the hinge location within the first and last quarter areas. Locate a pair of hinges an equal distance down from the top and up from the bottom.

Place a butt hinge against the frame and trace around it. Mortise the outlined area with a router and/or chisel so the hinge flange fits flush. Do the same on the door. Mark the screw locations and drill a proper pilot hole. Attach hinges to the loose door, then to the frame.

Magnetic latches work fine when the door opening faces either forward or aft. Athwartship openings require mechanical latches to keep cabinet doors closed when the boat heels.

REVIVING AND REPAIRING

Despite all your good efforts and intentions to refinish the wood on your boat, Mother Nature ultimately does her damage—and you are faced with some serious refurbishing. Exposure—especially to moisture—takes its toll on marine finishes and, eventually, on the woods on your boat. The ever-present high humidity of a boat's natural environment, salt spray, rain, and freshwater baths all conspire to lift finishes, raise grain, and promote mildew and her nasty cousin, wood rot. Water droplets act like tiny magnifying glasses to concentrate the sun's harmful rays or, when the sun favors the other hemisphere, freezing moisture expands and causes wood to check and crack. It's not pretty.

And although salt water helps preserve wood against rot, the flip side is that dried-on salt deposits form small prisms that concentrate sunlight and cause varnish to break down sooner.

To prevent severe problems and to maintain its inherent strength and beauty, wood needs to be protected from the elements. Unless you are new to boat ownership, you already know that keeping varnish up doesn't mean taking the finish back to bare wood each time you varnish. Usually, maintaining varnish means "only" having to clean, lightly sand (to provide some "tooth") and apply a fresh coat to bring the surface back to a bright luster. Regularly varnishing your brightwork will prolong the life of the wood trim, although maintaining a lot of brightwork can seem like painting the Golden Gate Bridge: once you reach landfall across the span, it's time to go to the other end and start again.

Unfortunately varnish does age, and eventually it will crack. When that happens the old varnish must be completely removed, the wood sanded and maybe bleached, and new varnish applied to protect the wood. Teak is the exception to the rule—it's the one wood that doesn't require a protective coating.

Teakwood contains natural oils and has a closed cellular structure that withstands the elements. As it weathers it self-seals and oxidizes to a gray color some boatowners prefer and many find acceptable. Periodic scrubbing is all that is required, although an occasional sanding may be needed to keep the weathering surface smooth. Holystone (sandstone) has been used for centuries to smooth teak decks without removing too much wood with each treatment. Although teak resists rot, it can dry out, so some oiling or other treatment might be necessary over time.

Repairing wood is more challenging than revarnishing, but it's doable with a few tools and the willingness to take on the task.

REFURBISHING OLD WOOD

Wooden boat trim often shows the ravages of wet and wear. The finish, when exposed to weather for too long, lets go. Shrinking wooden plugs lose their seal, and winter ice jacks them from their holes. Years of chafing, or maybe just cumulative scraping and sanding, abrades the surface to the point that refurbishment is in order.

MATERIALS AND TOOLS

Refurbishing generally follows most of the same finishing conventions as for new wood, with one exception: extra steps are required to restore the wood to uniform color and a smooth surface. A few specialty products can make the task easier.

Limited finishing instructions are included here to provide adequate information to complete the projects, but this book is about woodworking, not wood refinishing. For a comprehensive step-by-step look at refinishing, *Sailboat Refinishing* (part of The International Marine Sailboat Library) is recommended reading.

- **Bleach:** Oxalic acid is available in crystals or pre-mixed at pharmacies or chandleries. In high concentrations, oxalic acid bleaches blemishes and discoloration from wood surfaces. Two-part bleaching agents are also available.

  The second component of two-part bleaching agents is a neutralizer. Oxalic acid should be neutralized with soda ash or borax, although thorough flushing with water may be adequate. Acid bleach dissolves the softer wood cells, and saturating raw wood causes the fibers to swell. Resand before applying the finish.

- **Penetrating Epoxy:** Use this thin epoxy to fill deteriorated cells in small areas of rot. Since you want as much wicking as possible, penetrating epoxy works best if you can treat the end grain. Flood the epoxy well into the end fibers.

- **Sanding Sealer:** Sanding sealer protects new or newly exposed wood from glue discoloration. A light coat on adjacent areas—not on the surfaces to be glued—will help you wipe off errant adhesive.

- **Filler Stains:** Weathered wood and porous species may require a bit of filler stain to get the surface back to bright. Highly porous Philippine mahogany benefits from a coat of sealer *under* the filler stain. Color cards are helpful, but for true color penetration and match, test the stain on an inconspicuous spot that has been well prepped. Red mahogany filler stain is VERY red, almost cherry, which probably matches nothing on your boat.

- **Teak Products:** Products for teak probably occupy more chandler shelf space than all other wood protection products combined. Various sealers are intended to slow the loss of teakwood's natural oils. Supplemental oil products are available to renew the wood. One- and two-part cleaners nearly miraculously restore teak's golden color. Cleaners formulated for teak should *not* be used on other woods.

- **Varnish:** An advantage that varnish has over paint is that it lets you monitor any change in wood color beneath the coating. Your choices include varnishes of various hardness (known as length—short, medium, and long, depending on the amount of resin-to-oil mixed with the resin), varnishes that contain UV additives, and polyurethane-based varnishes for high-traffic areas.

  Soft (long) varnish is more elastic and waterproof than the harder variety. Sometimes called spar varnish, with a UV additive it's your choice for exterior wood. Polyurethane vanishes once tended to yellow wood; however, today's crystal-clear polyurethanes are a good choice for cabin soles and companionway ladders.

- **Solvents:** The coating that you choose will specify the solvent that's required for thinning, and the same thinner can be used for cleaning up. To clean a varnish brush, for example, use three containers: A first bath in mineral spirits removes most of the varnish from the brush; a second bath in clean spirits dissolves most remaining residue; a final bath in lacquer thinner leaves the bristles squeaky clean. Wipe and spin dry. If you allow the used solvent to stand, the suspended varnish will soon settle out and you can pour off the clean thinner for reuse. Follow good disposal procedures for the remaining semisolid sediment.

- **Brush-Flow Additives:** Manufacturers of coatings usually recommend their own brush-flow product. For general use, Penetrol is a good flow enhancer for most varnishes and paints. Even when the conditions are perfect, a little Penetrol will aid brush flow and improve results.

- **Brushes:** Experienced boat refinishers can use a rag to wipe on varnish to perfection, but don't try this on your own boat. Others swear by foam throwaway brushes and get stunning results. For the rest of us, a good-quality natural bristle brush is most likely to yield the best finish. Always brush varnish with the grain. The mantra of a good varnisher is "work to a wet edge."

SANDPAPER 101

Large surfaces are best finished with a palm sander, and for flat surfaces the sandpaper should be wrapped around a block, but for hand sanding irregular surfaces, how you fold the sandpaper can make a difference.

- The smooth back surface of a single sheet of sandpaper slips and slides in your hand more than it works against the wood.
- A single fold in the sheet feels inconsistent. Near the fold you have control over the sanding action, but the farther away from the fold you work, the more slippage you will experience.

But add a second fold and voilá!—an abrasive side against the smooth back surface reduces slippage, and the folds closer together add rigidity. As a result, a bifolded sheet cuts quicker and provides a better feel for what you're sanding. Use all three surfaces by folding the used panel to the inside when it loses its abrasion.

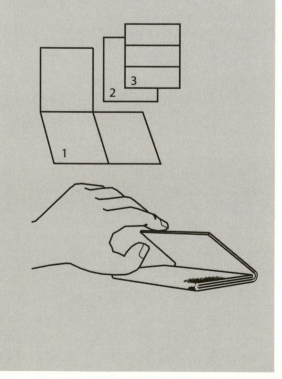

BACK TO BARE WOOD

Do your boat a huge favor by leaving your heavy disk and belt sanders at home. These tools are fine for stripping house paint or surfacing floors, but they are almost certain to do more harm than good on your boat. You need a light touch—and the right tools and materials—to restore damaged wood to its original beauty.

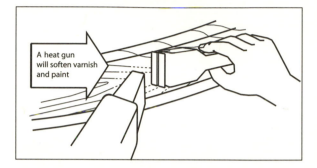

A heat gun will soften varnish or paint for a scraper to remove. Always work with the grain to minimize lifting the wood's fibers. A scraper with a wood handle won't conduct the heat to your hands. Be careful not to overheat surrounding fiberglass surfaces.

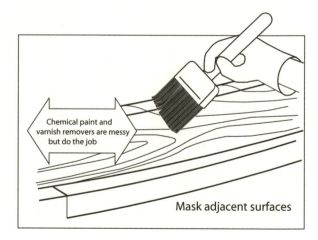

Chemical paint and varnish removers are messy but effective. They will dissolve almost any coating and can damage bare fiberglass, so you must mask adjacent surfaces and be certain no remover can penetrate this barrier.

Some removers are harsh but fast acting. Others, especially water-based products, take longer to work but are not quite as destructive to the applicators—meaning you and whatever you are using to spread the stuff.

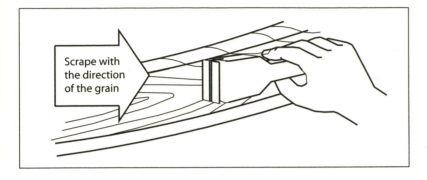

After the varnish (or paint) has been removed, some finish scraping readies the wood for sanding.

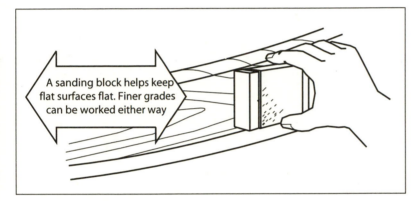

Block sanding.

Use a sanding block to keep flat surfaces flat. An initial grit of 120 should be coarse enough for most surfaces; follow that with 180- and 220-grit. Finer grits can be worked in any direction. Don't go too fine; you want to leave the wood with enough tooth (although invisible) for a good bond with the varnish.

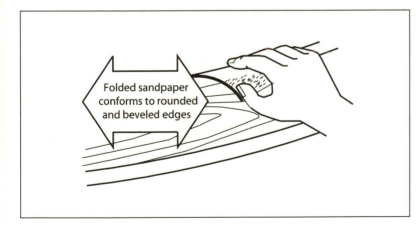

Finish sanding.

Use folded sandpaper and a light touch to sand rounded or broken (slightly beveled) edges.

ROT

The dreaded R-word isn't always that dreadful and doesn't always stand for "replace." Before you dive into a major removal and replacement project, look at how successfully the piece might be restored in place. My wise father-in-law said "a boat is a rusting, rotting thing, anyway." And an acquaintance of mine categorizes discoloration as "added character." But even with such eminently practical views, both would allow that nice brightwork is a pleasure to behold (but never a pleasure to attain).

Mildew is usually surface grown and rarely damaging. Fungus, mold, and bacteria are more serious because they feed on the wood itself—which results in surface blemishes and, if ignored, maybe dry rot. Damage can happen quickly, especially when temperatures and moisture levels are on the high side. You can wipe these unsightly and potentially damaging parasites off the surface of wood with a detergent and (chlorine) bleach solution.

Rot comes in two convenient forms. White rot consumes most of the wood fibers—and the color of the wood—as it spreads. Brown rot attacks only the cellulose, leaving the cell walls intact but hollow and weakened. Brown rot is also called dry rot, although it requires moisture to sustain growth and decay.

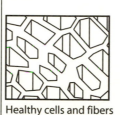  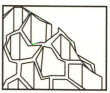

Healthy cells and fibers   Brown rot ignores cell walls   White rot consumes all

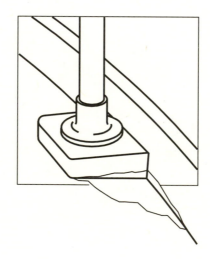

Rot, which breaks down the cellulose structure in wood, usually occurs where fresh water from rain, hoses, or condensation collects. Recurring wetness and high temperatures speed the decay process; air slows it. Good ventilation helps wood stay dry and healthy, a point to keep in mind as you plan modifications for your boat.

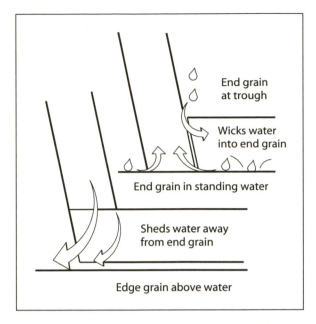

End grain
at trough

Wicks water
into end grain

End grain in standing water

Sheds water away
from end grain

Edge grain above water

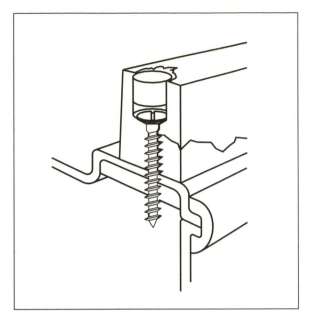

On wooden boats, rot sometimes migrates into adjacent pieces; on fiberglass boats, it is likely to be confined to the piece of wood where it originated. Even where wood is against wood, conditions for rot may not be present in an adjacent piece.

Other conditions cause wood to stain and decay. Oxidation of metal fasteners can create chemical stains. Where raw wood is left exposed to weather, the wood itself can oxidize over time.

REPAIRING ROT DAMAGE

Rot can seriously reduce the structural integrity of wood. If the decay is in a piece of wood that serves a function more vital than decorative trim, replacement is probably a priority. Minor rot damage can be repaired *in situ*.

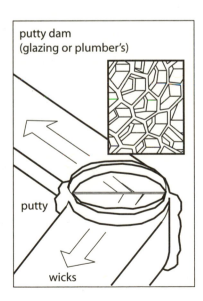

putty dam
(glazing or plumber's)

putty

wicks

If you discover the damage early, treating it with a penetrating epoxy can arrest or, at least, impede further decay and restore the wood cells at the same time (but probably not 100 percent). Smith's Penetrating Epoxy is a two-part, highly fluid mix that soaks into damaged wood fibers. Smith's slow cure rate allows multiple soakings for good coverage, although the deepest penetration occurs with the first application. Git Rot is a similar product, but sets up more quickly. Both of these products work best if you can flood the damaged area, allowing the epoxy to wick into open capillaries in the surrounding wood to seal the damage and, with luck, starve the decay.

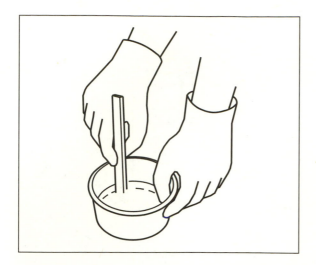

Some epoxy products carry health warnings, and with good reason. A significant number of people get an uncomfortable skin rash when they're exposed to epoxy, so always wear gloves when working with the stuff and keep it off your bare skin. Epoxy causes an exothermic reaction (it generates its own heat through a chemical process), and if you mix up a large batches in an unsuitable container, it can ignite or melt and make one hell of a mess.

REPAIR PROJECTS

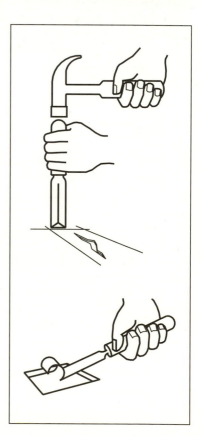

When a wooden part is structural and the damage has reduced its strength, the safest course is always replacement. But the wood isn't always weakened. Sometimes the damage only scars the surface or the wood has merely changed shape. These problems can't be cured with a fresh coat of varnish, or even an application of epoxy, but most can be handled by the weekend woodworker sailor.

THE DUTCHMAN

You dropped a wrench while doing some work aloft, and now you must pay for your folly. A dutchman (and maybe even a Dutchman) can repair gouges, dings, and chafing. The damage is simply chiseled out and replaced with a thin inlay of wood of the same species, color, and texture.

Use a straight chisel and a hammer to cut a square or rectangle surrounding the damaged area. Chisel out the rectangle to a constant depth—like cutting a mortise for flush-mounting a piece of hardware.

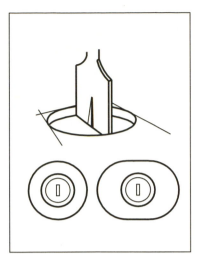

A small damaged area may sometimes be repaired with a circular or oval patch. Make the cutout with a spade bit. A patch of contrasting grain figuring or direction might be designed into a repair of, for instance, damage around a keyhole.

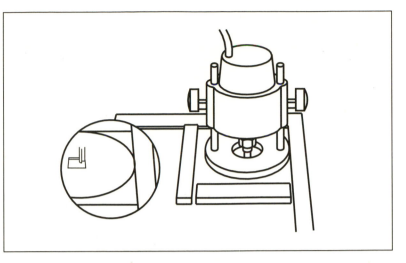

A router is also a good tool for cutting away damaged material. It has the advantage of cutting at a constant depth, providing a flat bottom surface for gluing the replacement piece.

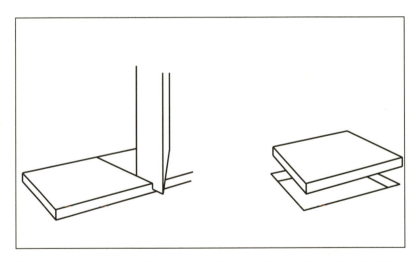

For the dutchman to match the surrounding wood, you will need to select the repair wood carefully. Take to your lumber supplier the largest piece of wood your chisel removes and match it as closely as possible in both color and grain. The patch should be slightly thicker than the cutout depth to make sure it can be sanded flush; use a chisel or router to shave a section of the replacement wood to the appropriate thickness. Sabersaw the patch from this area, paying attention to the grain. Pare the patch to size with your chisel, block sanding the edge for the final fit. Set the dutchman into the cutout with epoxy. When the glue is fully cured, sand the patch flush with the surrounding surface and apply the finish of choice.

STRAIGHTENING

Plywood and edge-joined planks are the two basic types of "flat" wood construction. They are used for doors, locker seats, and cabin soles. Plywood is relatively stable, but planks too often develop a twist or warp.

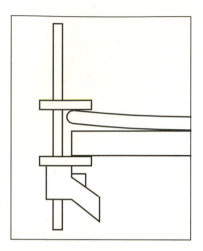

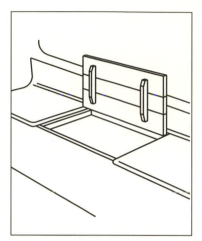

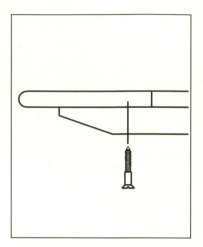

Use a straight cleat—called a strongback in this example—to reduce or eliminate warp in a plank or panel. You can test how effective a strongback will be by temporarily clamping the warped piece to a straight board (turned edgewise) to see if it will draw in with clamp pressure. Be aware that the joints of warped edge-glued panels may fail before the planks flatten.

A 1 x 2 used on edge is usually stiff enough to flatten a warped plank or panel. Strongbacks should extend as far across the panel as possible, taking into account surrounding frames, bulkheads, and whatever is installed or stowed beneath.

The ends of a strongback create abrupt lines of stress along the grain of the plank above. Reduce this "hard spot" by tapering the ends of the cleats.

Strip off any finish where the strongback will be installed so the glue can attach directly to the wood. Clamp the cleat in place and drill fastener holes well away from the glued joints. Countersink the holes for fasteners—which can be plugged if you wish. Mask adjacent areas, then release the clamps.

    This bond requires the strength and tenacity of epoxy. Apply the glue to both surfaces. Reclamp lightly, but seat and drive the screws home. Never rely on screws to bring pieces together. Excess epoxy can be wiped away with acetone or MEK. When correcting severe warp, allow extra curing time before removing the clamps.

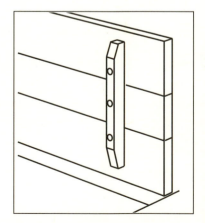

STRENGTHENING

Flat panels—plank or plywood—may be sound but too slight for their intended use. The deflection of a panel can be uncomfortable, disconcerting, and perhaps even dangerous. Strongbacks can stiffen a deflecting bilge hatch, strengthen flexing steps on a companionway ladder, or provide support where needed.

Panels

Well-placed and securely fastened strongbacks will stiffen a too-flexible panel and prolong its life. Where strongbacks to straighten warp are oriented in a single direction, flexible panels usually benefit from braces that run both lengthwise and crosswise. Taper the ends of strongbacks attached across the grain.

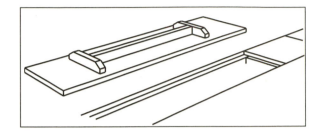

Ladders

A ladder rung that flexes when you step on it can be unnerving. We're not talking about ladders that are nearly unglued and ready to fall apart, but some companionway ladders could benefit from additional support across the tread or at the joints where the treads let into the sides.

If your companionway ladder could use a better nonskid surface, you can fasten raised slats or a grooved pad atop the rungs. Either addition is essentially a strongback mounted on top of the step rather than underneath, and both add stiffness to the step.

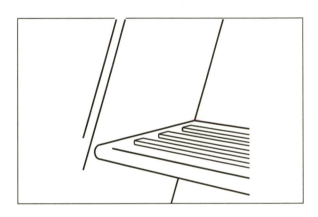

You can strengthen a ladder rung by attaching a strongback (called a riser when it supports a step) to the underside along the rear. Or you can fashion a decorative riser, shaped and sculpted, and install it closer to the nose of the step so your handiwork can be admired.

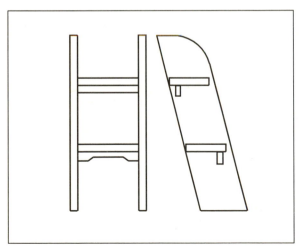

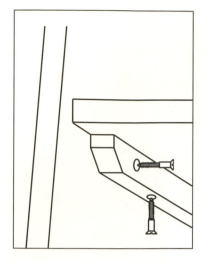

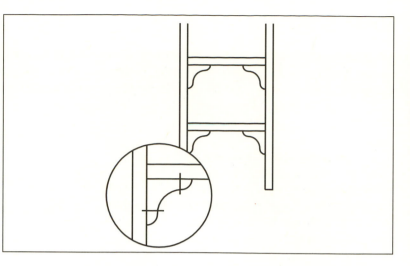

The area where the a step lets into the side rail is another potential weakness. Bolster this joint by adding cleats that are screwed and glued to the sides and rungs. These can be set back slightly from the nose of the rung with their exposed ends rounded or cut at a bevel—whichever better matches the existing design.

A gusset—a triangular bracket shaped to match the ladder design—can strengthen both the joint and the rung. It is usually best to mount the gussets close to the nose of the step. Gussets can be centered on the tread depth, but doing so might create a stress line by concentrating the full force of weight on the step beyond the fulcrum created by the gussets, or setback risers for that matter.

Cleats and gussets should be glued and screwed. For interior work, carpenter's glue should hold forever; exterior exposure suggests epoxy. Before gluing, position the pieces and drill pilot holes for the screws. Countersink for the screw heads, or counterbore and plug the holes if they are highly visible.

Select straight grain wood for strongbacks. Gussets, if a piece of random grain wood is unavailable, should be cut so the grain runs either parallel or perpendicular to the long side (hypotenuse) of the triangle. These grain orientations present a strong leg for fastenings in both directions. If the grain runs parallel to one short leg of the triangle, fasteners in the opposite leg will be in line with the grain, which is the worst possible orientation.

CROWNED SURFACES

Not all surfaces you might want to strengthen will be flat. If you want to add a strongback to a crowned surface such as a cabin overhead or hatch, read on.

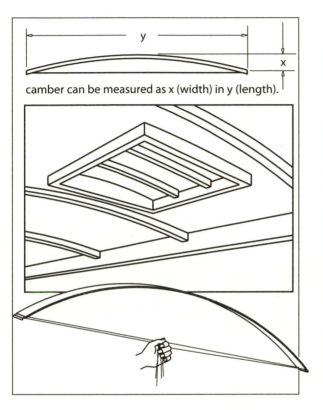

camber can be measured as x (width) in y (length).

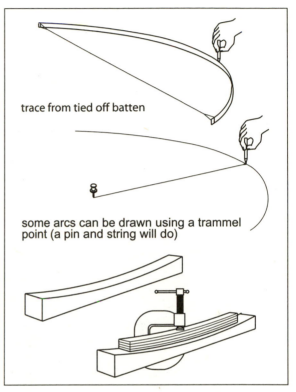

trace from tied off batten

some arcs can be drawn using a trammel point (a pin and string will do)

Use a piece of string to tie a thin batten into the appropriate curvature—like stringing a longbow. Transfer this curve to a piece of cardboard or thin plywood, then cut the pattern and check the fit. Measure twice, cut once.

Use the pattern to cut a curved strongback. Or, use it to cut a curved mold and laminate a strongback with the correct radius.

REMOVING AND REPLACING

When wood is damaged or weathered beyond any hope of refurbishing by bleaching, treating with penetrating epoxies, or patching in a dutchman, it may be time to remove and remake pieces. This might sound more drastic than repairing in place, but it isn't necessarily more complicated—and it offers the opportunity to improve the design of the damaged parts a bit. In fact, you might want to replace a part just to improve on its design, even though the original is still in fine condition.

Candidates for replacement projects include decorative pieces such as trim around lockers and open compartments, as well as the more functional wood parts that provide a base for hardware or a sacrificial surface to save other components from damage. Sacrificial wood, in particular, can become so scarred and worn that reworking is no longer an option and the whole piece should be replaced.

If you are happy with the shape and proportions of the old piece, use it for a pattern. But this is also an opportunity to widen or thicken the piece, miter the corners, quarter-round the edges, or make some other improvement over the original design. Just be sure the new piece looks like it belongs—the way the builder would have done it with more time, thought, or money.

Whether duplicating or redesigning, take special care not to alter the fit of the old piece where it mates with other components. And when replacing something that receives something else, such as companionway trim, maintain the width of guide slots so you don't alter the fit of the dropboards or other *gozinta* mating parts. An exact match of coloring and figuring is not as critical when replacing whole parts; close enough will be good enough.

EXTRACTING OLD SCREWS

Most trim pieces and other wooden components on a modern sailboat are attached with screws, which are often imbedded within the part and hidden beneath a wooden plug. With care—and some luck—you can extract these old fasteners without damaging the part they affix.

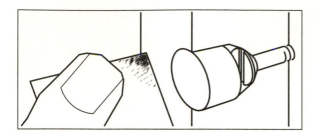

1 If there is any chance you'll want to reuse the re-moved part, be sure to strip the varnish from the area surrounding the plug. Varnish can form a membrane that is so tenaciously bonded to both the plug and surrounding member that it can lift and tear the wood around the hole.

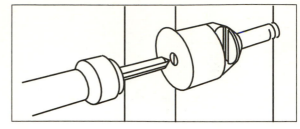

2 To remove the bung, start by drilling a small hole—$1/8$ inch is usually about right—through the center of the plug.

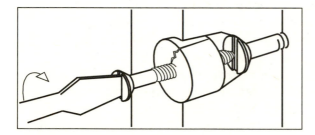

3 Drive a slightly larger wood screw (maybe a #8) into the drilled hole. If you're lucky, the plug will ride out on the screw threads when the screw contacts the old screw head below. Otherwise, it will probably split. You can pry it out with a punch or small nail, but be careful not to damage the surrounding edge. If you do damage the wood, you can drill for a larger plug back to good wood.

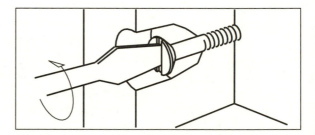

4 With the plug removed (or all the pieces picked out), back out the imbedded screw. It sometimes helps to rap old screws with a hammer through the screw-driver. This jars the threads and "awakens" the fas-tener, loosening it from its resting place.

REPLACING DECORATIVE TRIM

Of a boat's various wood components, decorative trim will generally be the easiest to remove and replace. Such items include wood frames around ports and other openings, corner moldings, eyebrows, and perhaps chafe rails. Let's get our feet wet by replacing the edge trim around a cockpit coaming pocket, which was damaged by some goofball with an errant wrench.

MATERIALS:

Wood, wood plugs, screws, polysulfide sealant

TOOLS:

Saw, drill, combination bit, sander, screwdriver

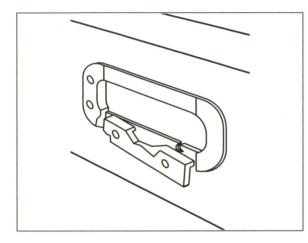

Following the steps above, remove the bungs and extract the fasteners to release the frame. If the frame was set in sealant, gently pry it free with a sharp putty knife.

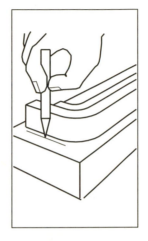

Trace the frame onto the new wood. The original may be an assembly of smaller components or it could have been fabricated in one piece.

Construct your replacement in whatever manner fits your skills and tools. To avoid exposing unweathered gelcoat, it is almost always better to keep widths the same or slightly oversized.

Cut out the parts with a sabersaw. You can cut a rabbet, which will hide the edge of the opening, into the new frame with a chisel or router. Clamp the molding between supporting and stop blocks to route the rabbet. If the frame needs to be grooved to slip over the thickness of the fiberglass, using a table saw will simplify the job. The parts of a grooved frame will have to be joined *after* they are installed.

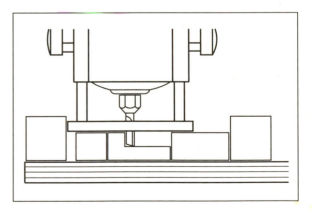

When refastening, you need to take into account the materials that the fasteners join and whether you will be using the old holes. Refastening wood to wood requires a different set of rules than when refastening wood to fiberglass.

WOOD TO WOOD

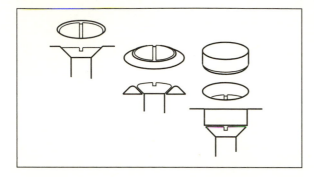

To fasten one wood component to another, use wood screws. A stainless steel or bronze flathead screw can be imbedded below a bung if the attaching piece is sufficiently thick. Otherwise, use a stainless steel oval-head screw set inside a stainless steel finishing washer. For out-of-sight, out-of mind locations, use a flathead screw set flush or slightly inset in a countersink.

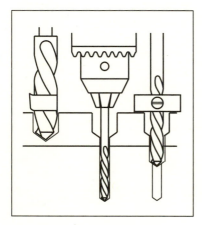

For imbedded screws, start by boring the hole for the bung. Bungs come in standard sizes—$1/4$, $3/8$, and $1/2$ inch—so select a diameter that will clear the screw head *and* the screwdriver blade so you can install the fastener without damaging the hole. The depth of the hole should be not less than half of the plug diameter, and it should have a chamfer at the bottom that matches the underside of the screw head. (The point of a twist drill will create this.)

Next, clamp or tape the attaching piece in position and drill a pilot hole, starting at the center of the counterbore, through the attaching piece and into the receiving piece. The pilot hole should be the core diameter of the screw or, in softer woods, slightly smaller. The depth—measured from the bottom of the counterbore—should be just short of the full length of the screw.

Finally, counterbore the pilot hole out to the shank diameter of the screw to a depth—measured from the bottom of the bung hole—equal to the length of the screw shank. Use a drill collar to stop at this depth, or place a piece of masking tape on the drill bit to mark the proper depth. The shank counterbore may need to extend into the receiving piece.

Or, make it easy on yourself and buy a combination bit that drills plug, shank, and pilot holes in a single operation. You can choose a bit that's designed just

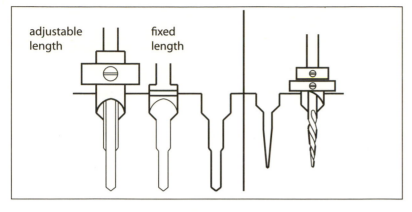

TAPERED BITS

Tapered bits approximate the shape of wood screws, so they provide good pilot holes in all but the hardest woods. But unless you have tapered drill bits on-hand, a set of regular twist drill bits will handle all your week-end woodworking needs nicely.

for your specific screw size—in both gauge and length—or you can select an adjustable bit that fits a specific screw diameter, but that lets you adjust for the depth of pilot holes and counterbores to accommodate screws of different lengths.

WOOD TO FIBERGLASS

Wood screws don't hold well in fiberglass. Even where fiberglass sheaths a wood core, the integrity of the plywood core is unknown and should not be relied upon. Trust the fiberglass and use self-tapping screws.

The recommended pilot hole diameters for installing self-tapping screws into fiberglass are general guidelines only. The correct hole size depends on the thickness and composition of the fiberglass. Some resistance is needed to keep the screw in place, but if the hole is too tight, you will twist the screw in half or, worse, fracture the fiberglass. Start with the drill size shown in the table, but if the screw is hard to turn, stop, and enlarge the hole slightly.

Any head type can be used to fasten wood into fiberglass, but if you are using pan- or round-head screws under bungs, the bottom of the counterbore should be flat instead of chamfered so the flat screwhead surfaces seat firmly when tightened.

You want the head of the screw to clamp the attaching piece tightly against the receiving surface. To prevent the wood from riding up on the screw threads, counterbore the hole through the wood to a slide fit for the screw. Since self-tapping screws are threaded from head to tip, the shank hole doesn't extend into the fiberglass.

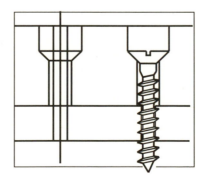

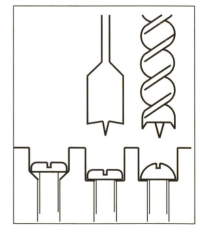

FIBERGLASS TO WOOD

Why, you might wonder, if this is a woodworking book, are we mounting something made of fiberglass? We aren't.

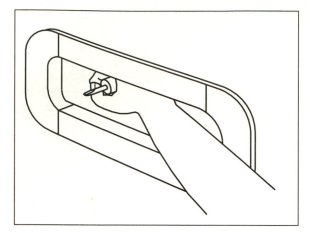

Sometimes it is easier to attach wood to fiberglass from behind. If you have access to the back side of the mounting surface, the face of the attached wood item can be left unmarred, and you won't have to use bungs.

Because the mounting screws will thread into wood, use wood screws. To seat flat against fiberglass, select screws that have a flat under the head—either round-head or pan-head. Oval-head screws, used with appropriate finishing washers, may be a better choice if the fasteners will be exposed.

Drill the hole through the fiberglass to a slip fit for the shank of the screw and counterbore the wood deep enough to accommodate the length of the shank extending into the wood.

OLD HOLES

It is usually preferable to redesign the hole pattern so the fasteners thread into fresh material. Sometimes, however, there's a good reason to use the same screw holes to reinstall a renovated or remade part. Only rarely can you also use the original fasteners with good results.

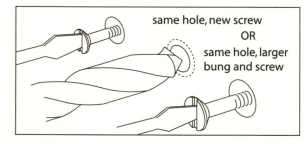

same hole, new screw
OR
same hole, larger bung and screw

Test the holes with a new screw of the same size before refastening in the same hole pattern. It is almost always safer to upsize the diameter. If there's enough depth behind for a longer screw, that can accomplish the same purpose. Don't just drive a larger screw into the old hole; redrill it with the appropriate bit for the new screw. This is particularly important when refastening into fiberglass.

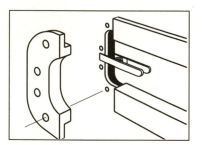

Backing plates, either glassed or epoxied in place, are another option when you are forced to reuse existing holes. Backing plates are most satisfactory when they are hidden. In a pinch, filling the hole with epoxy paste and redrilling it may be a satisfactory fix.

Larger screws may require more clearance and larger bungs. Plug size can also be enlarged to correct bunghole damage that may have occurred when removing or installing the fastener. Larger twist drills will self-center in the original hole. If you are using a spade bit, insert a bung to be drilled out with the longer hole.

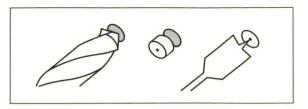

INSTALLING BUNGS

Plugs should be inserted so the grains line up (the grain of the plug matches that of the piece it is in). Screw plugs should be as inconspicuous as possible—a boat is not a pegged hardwood floor. Glue is not recommended unless that is all that will work. Using varnish to seat and seal the bung will allow it to be removed in the future.

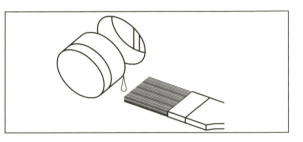

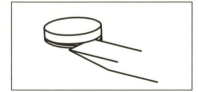

With the plug firmly set, place a chisel bevel (side down) at one end of the grain with the blade edge $1/16$ inch or so above the surrounding wood. Tap lightly but don't cut. A second tap from the opposite side should shear the head slightly proud in the hole. Chisel away the excess, leaving enough to be sanded flush.

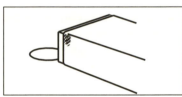

Use a sanding block to bring the bung flush with the surrounding surface, then finish sand the whole piece as if the bung weren't there.

You can buy plugs in teak and mahogany (and other woods) or you can buy a plug cutter and make your own. Plug cutters designed for use in a drill chuck come in a variety of standard sizes. Cut plugs perpendicular to the grain direction so they will pop free when pried with a screwdriver, and trim flat with the grain when chiseled. If you intend to cut many plugs, a drill press is suggested.

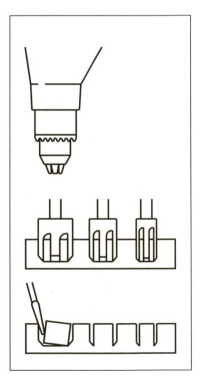

CABIN MOLDING

If the builder of your boat didn't do the kind of job below that elicits praise, your developing woodworking skills provide the opportunity to make improvements.

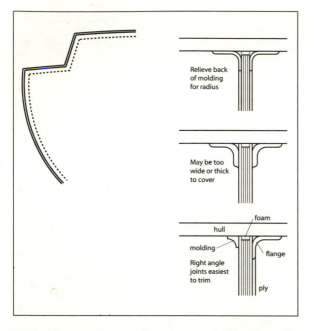

Relieve back of molding for radius

May be too wide or thick to cover

foam

hull

molding

flange

Right angle joints easiest to trim

ply

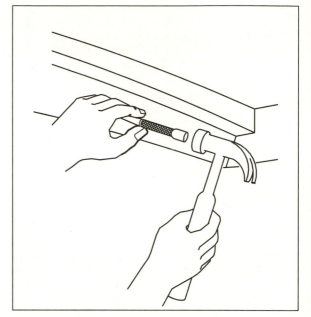

Bulkheads compartmentalize a boat and stiffen the hull. A properly installed bulkhead sits on a foam pad to prevent the unyielding plywood edge from interfering with the natural flex of the hull, thereby creating a hard line of stress. Bulkheads are typically bonded in place with fiberglass flanges that turn up onto the bulkheads and out onto the hull surface. The wider the flange, the stronger the joint—but super-size flanges are a challenge to cover with wooden molding. Molding must be undercut (with a beveled edge or chiseled) to clear the radius of the flange.

Before attempting to remove bulkhead molding, inspect it closely. Wood plugs tell you that the molding is screwed in place; extracting the plugs and removing the screws should release the molding. A pattern of dots of filler suggests that the molding is nailed in place. The easiest way to release the molding often is to drive the nails on through the molding with a thin nail set. If there is access to the back side of the installed trim, look there for fasteners. If you can't see the fasteners on the back side, it's likely that none are there because access was difficult when the trim was originally installed.

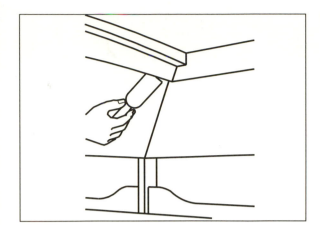

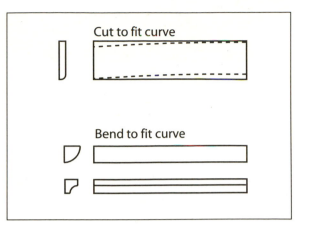

If the means of fastening is not obvious, the molding is probably attached with some type of adhesive. Removing bonded molding is an iffy proposition at best. You may be able to pry (or cut) the molding free with a sharpened putty knife, but the bond is sometimes stronger than the wood. Be sure you are prepared to make new molding before you try to remove a molding that is cemented in place.

When designing replacement trim, add a bit of width to the new work to hide the old joint line. Narrow moldings can be bowed to conform to the slight arc of the cabin-top or upper hull, but greater curvature needs to be cut into the molding. Don't expect to put any bend in wide molding; shape it to the required contour.

Corner angles of bulkhead trim are rarely square and require an extra step to determine the correct diagonal for a corner butt joint or the proper half-angle for a miter.

For a butt joint, use an adjustable bevel to transfer the corner angle to the ends of both sections of molding. Transfer this angle from the bevel to paper for a mitered corner. Bisect the angle by striking arcs from intersect A to points B and C. From points B and C, strike an arc slightly longer than lines A-B and A-C. A line from D (where these arcs intersect) back to A is a starting point for cutting the molding. The half angle will shift slightly if the molding bends to follow the curvature of the hull or overhead, so make only one of the cuts—not both—before fitting the molding pieces in place.

An alternative that avoids the geometry of butt or mitered corners and adds visual interest in the bargain is the use of a transition piece in the corner. You can follow nautical tradition by fashioning a corner piece with the look of a hanging knee.

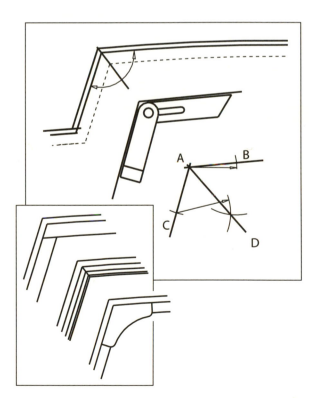

FUNCTIONAL TRIM

Ornamentation is technically a function, but here we are talking about wood components that serve as hardware bases, chafe protection, or perhaps to keep you aboard. The following projects are not all-inclusive but are representative of the steps required to make similar repairs on your vessel.

MATERIALS:

Wood, plugs, screws or bolts, epoxy, sealant

TOOLS:

Saw, Drill, drill bits, sander, screwdriver, wrench

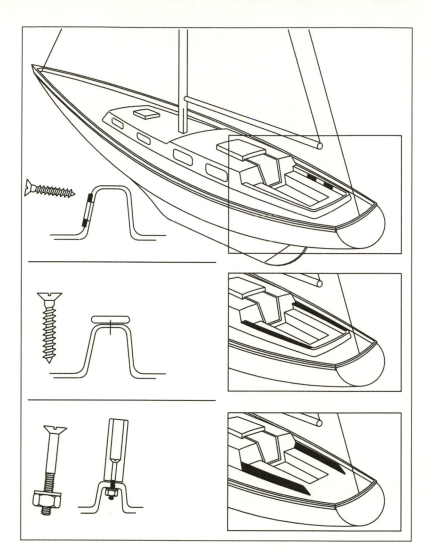

COCKPIT COAMING

There are as many different styles of cockpit coamings as there are cockpits. Some boats have molded coamings, some of which may be faced with wood on top and (less often) on the interior side. Other coamings are entirely wood, fastened at the bottom to a step in the deck and standing proud, usually with reinforcing winch pads behind. The sequence is the same for removing and replacing coamings and other functional wood components as it is for decorative trim, except that the wood may be sandwiched between hardware and the fiberglass structure of the boat, necessitating removal of the hardware. And, the wood itself is likely to be fastened with bolts rather than screws to withstand the stress and the load the piece is expected to carry.

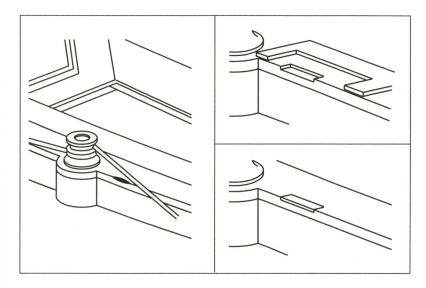

When the structural integrity of a piece is impaired, you may need to replace the piece entirely. When structural integrity isn't impaired, you may instead want to refurbish the existing part, especially when limited access makes total replacement difficult.

A router used with a template efficiently removes damaged wood to a uniform depth and creates a perfect perimeter edge ready for an inlay. Match the grain and color and "work" the new piece until you get a perfect fit. Bond the patch with epoxy, fair it, and refinish the entire piece.

COMPANIONWAY FRAME

After years of exposure and ham-fisted handling of dropboards, the damage to a companionway frame may be beyond hiding with extra coats of varnish.

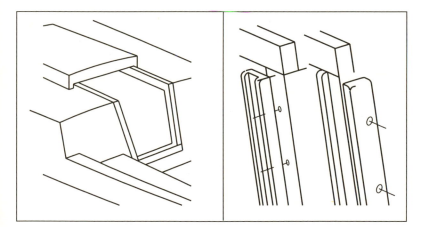

Removal is a matter of locating and drilling out the plugs, extracting the fasteners, and easing each part from its well-bedded, well-varnished position. You may have to remove the parts in a specific sequence; if so, remember it for reassembly.

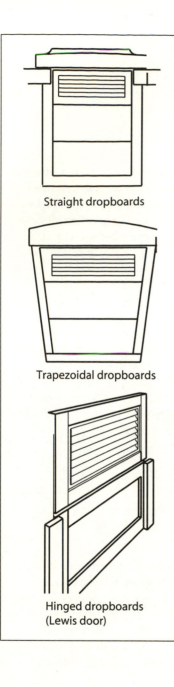

Straight dropboards

Trapezoidal dropboards

Hinged dropboards
(Lewis door)

The wood trim around a companionway is a natural focal point, so even if only one side needs replacing, do both for the sake of appearance. Remaking the trim also allows you to alter the width, thickness, and maybe even the threshold—but unless you also plan to replace the dropboards and the lock, be sure you maintain the width and position of the slot.

Look at the transition from the capturing molding to wooden chafe guards or other trim across the after face of the cabin trunk. Maybe your redesign will incorporate the other trim the molding fits into or complements.

DROPBOARDS

Dropboards can suffer as much damage as companionway frames because of their interaction and because they expose a larger face to the elements. Most dropboard damage, though, occurs not when they are in use but when they're sliding around loose in the cockpit or cabin as the boat pitches and heels.[*]

If you cut new dropboards, bevel, rabbet, or both, an interlocking step along mating edges outward and downward so water will sheet off when the boards are stacked in the slot. More bevel will be required for boards that do not sit vertical.

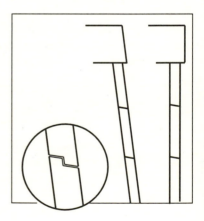

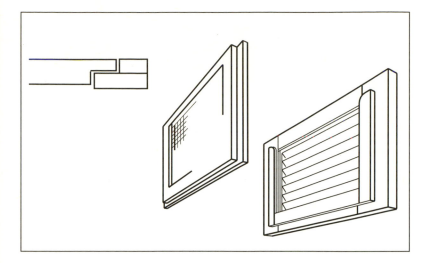

Adding a louvered panel (see Chapter 2) to a new or existing dropboard is a valuable improvement to almost any boat because it greatly improves air circulation when the boat is closed. For cold days aboard, add a slide-in panel behind the louvers to keep the heat in and the cold out. The same slot can also house a slide-in screen to keep bugs at bay when gunkholing in the summer swelter. Rabbet a slot for the insert or laminate two pieces to form the slot guide.

RUBRAILS

Rubrails stand between oncoming bumps and susceptible parts of the boat such as the hull, the deck joint, or the toerail. Because rubrails are meant to be sacrificial, they may periodically need to be repaired.

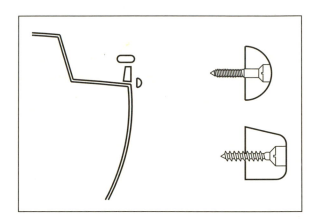

The rubrail on your boat may be an extruded rubber bumper in a stainless steel track fastened to the hull or deck, but if it is wood it might be a half-round bead or a more rectangular form that is angled or beveled to shed water. We aren't talking about replacing the full run—we're just going to repair the damaged sections.

TOERAILS

Toerails typically have dual functions: they hide the hull-to-deck joint and keep you from sliding over the side when the boat heels. Their outboard location subjects them to damage and their vertical orientation means they collect nightly dew and all-day sun. Damaged and/or deteriorated toerails are not uncommon sights.

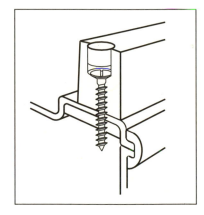

Although rubrails are attached around the sheerline of a boat, toerails may be more integral with the deck, hardware, or deck joint. Therefore, toerails are a little more challenging to fix or alter. Because they are on top, the bungs in toerails often split or shrink, thereby letting moisture into the holes.

CAPRAILS

Caprails present a whole new series of problems because they need to curve across their wide dimension. That means the curvature is usually cut into them rather than bent.

If caprails are a part of your wood trim, chances are they were the handiwork of an experienced shipwright who could shape, hew, and fair wood. The weekend woodworker may be able to resurface a caprail or inlay a dutchman on one, but for projects beyond that, it may be time to call in the pros.

SCARF JOINTS

A butt joint used to join the ends of two pieces of wood does not provide lateral strength. To get good strength at the joint you need the two pieces to overlap, which is accomplished by cutting the ends on matching diagonals.

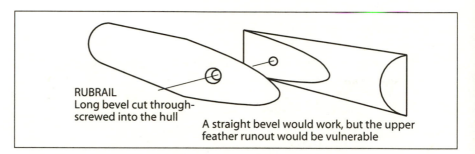

RUBRAIL
Long bevel cut through-screwed into the hull

A straight bevel would work, but the upper feather runout would be vulnerable

The simplest scarf joint is a continuous bevel. Its length should be at least six times the height of the joined pieces (not as drastic as the recommended 12 to 1 for planking and plywood). This type of scarf joint is fine for joining sections of a rubrail. If you have a choice, the feathered edge should always point aft to reduce the potential for snagging as the boat moves forward. A mounting screw through the middle of the scarf serves two purposes: it captures the joint and connects the piece.

A boxed scarf eliminates the feathered edge. The toerail should be joined with a box scarf or, better yet, a lock scarf. A pair of screws through the scarf joint and into the deck helps to stabilize the joint.

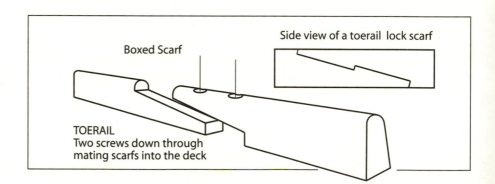

Side view of a toerail lock scarf

Boxed Scarf

TOERAIL
Two screws down through mating scarfs into the deck

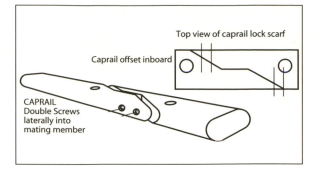

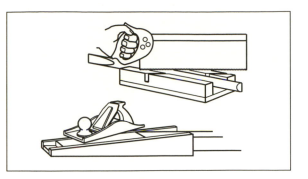

This is one example of how an existing scarf joint might be fashioned. A scarf joint between sections of caprail should be oriented across the rail. The length, and consequently the strength, can be increased by putting a step in the middle of the joint. Use double screws at each end of the joint to fasten the pieces together, then install mounting screws just beyond the joint on both ends to reduce stress on the joint.

Cutting out the damaged portion of a rubrail or toerail may require fashioning a cutting jig to guide your saw, plane, or router. Using plywood wedges flanking the piece as guides will help you plane a smooth beveled edge. A special "skinny" miter box knocked together from scrap wood can let you cut matching bevels with a backsaw.

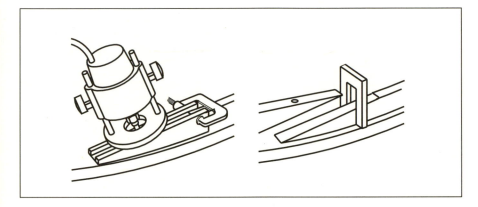

Confined damage can be repaired by "scarfing in" a short section of replacement rail. Ideally, this requires no more than cutting out a V-section and dropping a new piece into place. If the damage is near the bow or stern, replacing the wood to the end may be better and easier because it limits the repair to a single scarf.

Cutting a V-section from a rail that is attached to a boat requires extra care to protect the fiberglass. Loosen the rail beyond the damaged section enough to slip a protective cardboard between your cut and the fiberglass. Cut to the rough shape, then clamp flanking wedges to guide the plane or router.

The replacement section should be long enough to fair the piece to the run of the rail. Short patches should be from thicker stock so the "line" can be faired in to the run.

Have plenty of clamps (and protective pads) handy, and cut some plywood clamps to fit the width of the rail to hold the piece in place for final fitting (the bevel may change with the bend) and fastening.

Grabrails are an essential part of your boat's safety gear. The easiest (and sometimes least expensive) way to add a new grabrail is to buy one from your favorite chandler. But when you need to replace an existing grabrail, an "off-the-shelf" rail is probably not your best alternative.

MATERIALS:

1 x 6 board (teak or mahogany recommended), wood plugs, bolts, polysulfide sealant

TOOLS:

Drill, hole saw, sabersaw, router, sander, screwdriver, wrench

Your first challenge (unless you own a wooden boat, which is the ultimate first challenge) is to gain access to the fasteners. Too often, manufacturers install cabintop grabrails before the headliner is in place—in total disregard for the inevitable. Broken or untrustworthy grabrails must be replaced, regardless of the difficulty.

A soft headliner is sometimes not too difficult to detach (start at one end of it). If it can't be detached, find each grabrail fastener by feel and cut a small access hole. To locate fasteners behind a molded headliner, you may have to break the grabrail free and then drill tiny positioning holes next to the screws through the deck and liner. Later, you will cover access holes in both soft and hard headliners with small wood pads that also serve as backing plates. Or, you can hide them with matching grabrails inside the cabin.

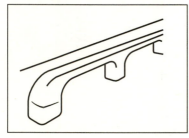

You don't need to be told this, but grabrails should never be pieced or patched. Any grabrail that requires more than cosmetic repair must be replaced. Period.

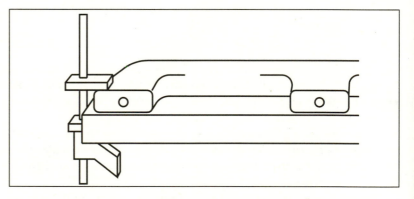

The biggest advantage to making your own grabrails is that you can re-use the original mounting holes pattern that's already drilled through the deck. Clamp the old handrail flat to your board and trace its outline.

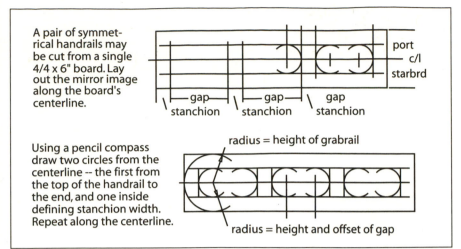

A pair of symmetrical handrails may be cut from a single 4/4 x 6" board. Lay out the mirror image along the board's centerline.

port
c/l
starbrd

gap | stanchion
gap | stanchion
gap | stanchion

Using a pencil compass draw two circles from the centerline -- the first from the top of the handrail to the end, and one inside defining stanchion width. Repeat along the centerline.

radius = height of grabrail

radius = height and offset of gap

Even if only one grabrail is damaged, replacing them in pairs assures a good color match and lets you alter the original design to add strength—and perhaps length. Draw a line down the exact center of your board and lay out the grabrails as mirror images on either side of that centerline. If you decide to add matching grabrails to the cabin overhead, mirror-cutting will ensure that they are a perfect fit.

Rather that trace the old grabrail, lay it against the centerline and mark off the stanchion locations. Use these marks as starting points to lay out height, width, and distance between stanchions for the new grabrails. Use a pencil compass on the centerline to give all the stanchions the same radius, which is determined by how thick you want the grip. Also swing an arc from outside edge to outside edge to define the ends of the grabrails.

Chuck a circle cutter or hole saw in your drill and cut out the circles you have drawn on the centerline of the board. Use a sabersaw to cut the radius on the ends and to cut between pairs of circles to create grip cutouts.

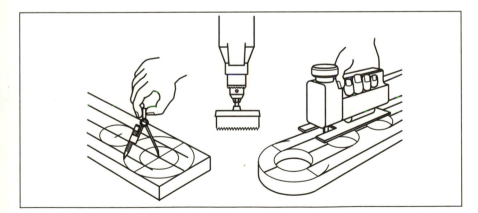

Load a shouldered quarter-round bit into your router and run it over all edges, then turn the board over and do it again to remove all corners and give the grip a comfortable oval shape. Using a router is much easier than rasping away anything that isn't handrail.

Rip the board on the centerline into two matching grabrails.

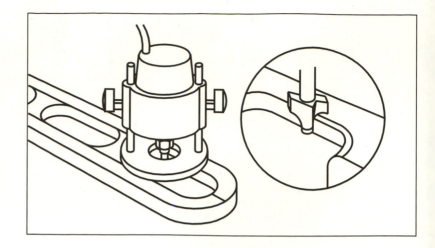

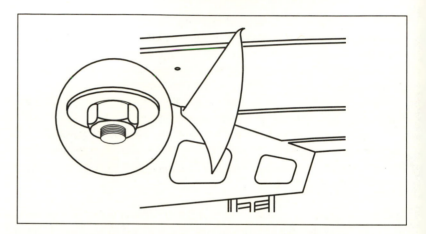

Proper installation of grabrails requires that they be through-bolted—at least at each end. Long wood screws driven from below might be used to fasten the middle stanchions, but bolting all will add security. Self-tapping screws driven into the fiberglass are totally inadequate for secure installation.

While a helper holds each stanchion in position—and temporarily inserts fasteners as you go—drill each fastener hole from below, using the existing mounting hole as a guide. A straight rail can be given a bit of curvature during attachment to parallel the cabinside. Bed the stanchions in polysulfide sealant and fasten.

LAMINATED TILLERS

A tiller is essentially a stick that turns a rudder. Any stick might do, but since a tiller is a tactile connection to our boat, most of us want our tiller to be exceptional. It must also be strong enough to handle its considerable load, have a comfortable grip, and be the right height and length for you. If you steer with a wheel, you can take this weekend off and go sailing.

MATERIALS:

Resawn (thin) plies of two contrasting woods, epoxy, hardware from old tiller

TOOLS:

Gluing fixture, clamps, files, plane, sander

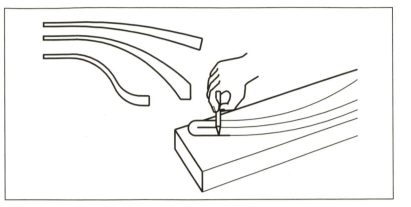

Tillers don't need to be laminated—one that's fabricated from solid lumber might be fine for your boat. Sailors sometimes carve tillers from clear ash baseball bats or hickory ax handles, but a laminated tiller, when glued properly, will be stronger for its size than one made from a single hunk of wood. Whichever construction you choose, use the existing tiller as your pattern, correcting any shortcomings in length, height, or clearance.

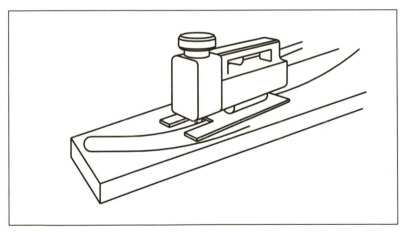

Laminating a tiller is essentially a process of cutting out eight or ten thin tiller shapes and gluing them together into the desired thickness. You have the option of using a single wood species or alternating light- and dark-colored strips—traditionally mahogany and ash, but almost any hardwood might be used.

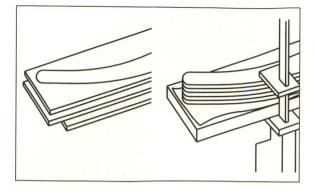

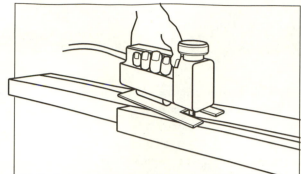

If you use vertical plies, cut each ply to the desired contour, then glue them together against a straight surface. Since the plies don't have to bend, you can use 1/4-inch or thicker stock—thicker plies give more definition to the layers.

A tiller that dips, dives, or sweeps into an *S* should be laminated with horizontal plies, which requires a fixture to form the laminates while they are being glued together.

Trace the tiller contour onto a sheet of kraft or butcher paper. Draw a straight line from end to end, then flank it with two parallel lines that clear the curve by at least $1/2$ inch. The width between these two lines is the board width you need to make the fixture. If you don't have a scrap piece of two-by stock wide enough, edge glue 2 x 4s or 2 x 6s to get sufficient width where you need it. Transfer the contour to the wood and cut it with a sabersaw.

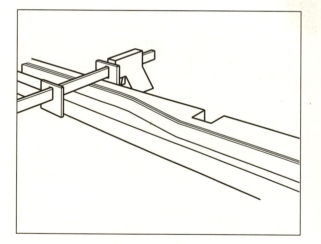

The amount of bend dictates how thin the laminates can be. Eighth-inch strips will conform to a fairly severe bend under clamping pressure; for less curvature, use thicker wood. Dry-fit a test strip in the fixture before committing to that thickness.

Buy the wood already milled to the thickness you need. Select a width that will net one ply (without too much spoilage), or cut multiple plies side by side from a wider board. Remember that the kerf (the width of the saw blade cut) reduces the useable width of the board with every cut.

Eighth-inch stock can be hard to come by, and expensive when you find it. You might want to befriend a woodworker with a band saw or table saw to resaw some stock to a workable thickness. A fine-toothed blade will produce a cut that can be glued with epoxy and filler, or you can block sand the resawn surfaces for bonding with unthickened epoxy.

Have all materials and clamps ready for the assembly. Cover the base and the edges of the clamping fixture with waxed paper or a generous coat of paste wax that contains Carnuba. Mix the epoxy resin and hardener—only the amount you can use before it goes off—and thicken it with the filler to the consistency of catsup. Brush the thickened epoxy onto the mating surfaces of several plies and clamp them into the fixture. Use sufficient clamps to get the lamination to seat fully. The laminates may tend to slide around, so be watchful and/or add clamps across the laminates to prevent this.

Since you have to release the clamps to add additional laminates, let the epoxy set before proceeding. Thicker amounts of epoxy generate more heat, so the epoxy in the container will harden first—but the epoxy that's between plies won't be far behind. While you are waiting, scrape off excess epoxy that clamping squeezed out.

When you are sure the first mix is set, mix up a fresh batch of epoxy and add several plies to those already bonded, removing and replacing the clamps. Continue this process until the full thickness is achieved, then leave the laminations under clamp pressure for 24 hours to fully cure.

USING EPOXY

Epoxy comes in two parts—resin and hardener—and it is critical that you mix them in the specified proportions. Inexpensive metering pumps are highly recommended—they take the guesswork and uncertainty out of mixing. If you have a choice, select a slow hardener to give you more "open" time to adjust the plies.

Pure epoxy has poor gap-filling properties. Either microfibers or colloidal silica will thicken the epoxy sufficiently to fill narrow voids in the laminate while maintaining good bond strength.

In addition to epoxy and filler, you will need rubber gloves, suitable mixing containers, stir sticks, disposable brushes, and acetone for cleanup.

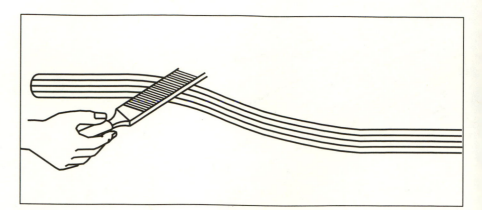

Whether shaping a laminated form or a blank you cut from solid wood, round over the edges to rough in the shape with a rasp, Surform, or block plane.

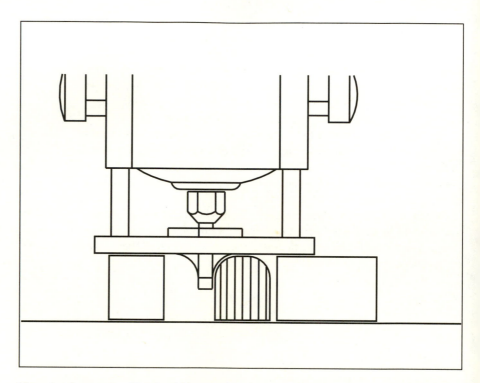

The grip of your new tiller should be comfortable. Its end can be more rounded than the rest of the stick. Use a router with a shouldered quarter-round bit to bring the end into shape. Use a stopblock so the router can cut transitions into the more rectangular shape the same distance from the tip.

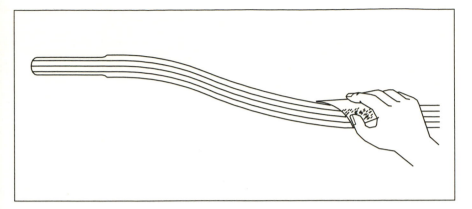

Use progressively finer sandpaper around a sanding block or in your palm sander to first fair (100-grit), then to smooth (120- to 180-grit), and finally to prepare for varnishing (220-grit). Be sure to wipe well after sanding with coarser grits to remove heavier abrasive bits that are left behind. Finish with varnish as described on pages 27 or 44.

WOOD PROJECTS FROM SCRATCH

By now, if you have assembled a prefabricated kit from your chandler, done a bit of repair and replacement of existing wood parts on your boat, or all of the above, you will have experienced a good sampling of joinery and assembly methods. Becoming comfortable with these woodworking techniques has direct application for projects you construct from scratch.

This section presents a sampling of weekend projects you can make from scratch. They begin with items cut and carved from solid wood, progress onto simple lumber and plywood assemblies, and end up with some basic joinery work for building boxes and cases.

None of these projects is beyond the skill of the weekend woodworker. They may take longer than you anticipate and, in the end you may believe that they're somehow flawed, but they are almost certain to result in useful additions to your boat. With each project, your woodworking skills will improve.

These designs are open to *your* interpretation—they are an assortment of generic projects you can tailor to your boat and woodworking interests. The suggested joinery can be more elaborate with each project your build.

Once you become more comfortable (say confident) with saw, drill, plane, and sander, you will be ready to launch future projects single-handed.

ONE-PIECE PROJECTS

You can sculpt some very useful boating gear from a solid block of wood. Of course, getting an adequately dimensioned block often requires laminating, so "one-piece" might be a bit of a misnomer, but it does best describe projects that involve little or no assembly.

MATERIALS:

Solid or laminated teak blocks, plugs, mounting fasteners

TOOLS:

Saw, drill, drill bits, sanding drum, finishing sander

DECK CHOCKS

Almost any item carried on deck will be more secure if it is stowed in chocks custom designed for both the item and its location on deck. The best chocks will both position and secure the items they are designed to hold.

Deck-mounted chocks should be bedded in sealant and screwed to the fiberglass deck or through-bolted if holding heavy gear.

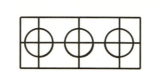

lash holes for heavy weather

Use a hole saw to fabricate a pair of cradles for your whisker pole. If the pole has a large diameter, cut the chocks with a sabersaw. A small drum sander in your power drill will speed shaping and finish sanding.

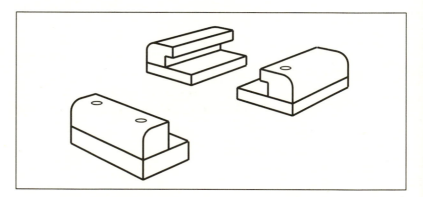

An anchor can be held in place on deck with strategically placed chocks that capture the flukes and heel of the anchor. Such chocks can be either three-layer laminated assemblies of varying widths or two layers with the upper board given a rabbet to fit the flukes.

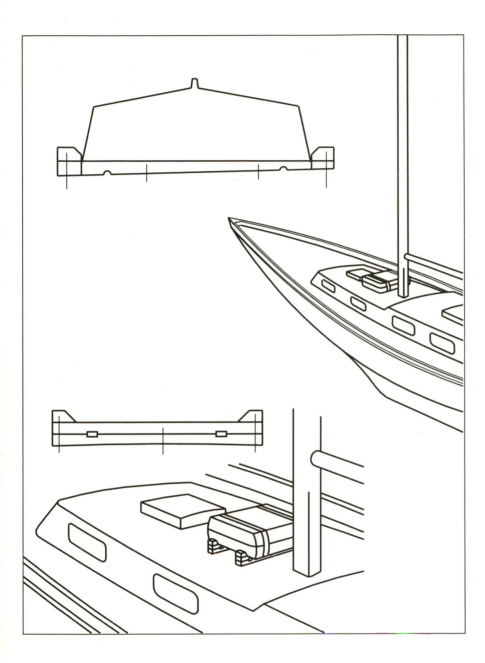

If you are fortunate enough to have the on-deck space to carry your dink on board, consider a teak-laminated assembly. The support portion could be tapered to the slant (if any) of the cabin trunk, but a cradle that is parallel to the deck works also because an inverted dinghy doesn't need to be stowed flat. Drain holes in the fore-and-aft cleats will aid water runoff and in athwartship cleats are essential to prevent water from collecting.

For a liferaft mount, follow the same construction method as above. Cut the lower laminate to the camber of the cabin trunk. To level the canister fore and aft, make one chock taller than the other.

Through-holes are for 1-inch nylon tie-down straps. Use quick release cinches or cut the straps with a knife.

ENSIGN POLE

With a plane, a rasp, and some sandpaper, you can facet the four corners of a length of square stock to form a handsome and unusual octagonal ensign staff.

MATERIALS:

Wood (teak or mahogany)

TOOLS:

Saw, plane, rasp, palm sander

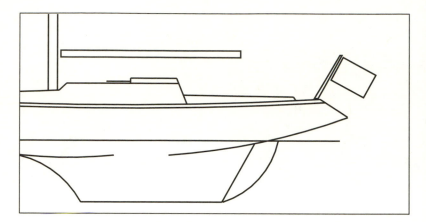

An ensign should be at least 1 inch on the fly per foot of boat length. Yacht ensigns and national colors have a ratio of about two-thirds height-to-length, so the pole should be at least as long as the flag; $1\frac{1}{3}$ flag length is even better.

Use $1\frac{1}{4}$-inch square stock for a 24- to 30-inch staff and $1\frac{1}{2}$-inch for longer poles. Buy stock a bit longer than the finished pole so you can cut off checked or split ends. Be sure the wood is close grained and homogeneous so it will plane easily.

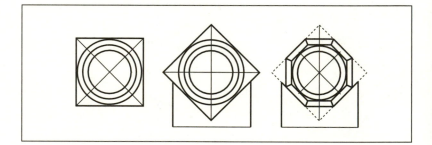

Draw crosshairs from corner to corner on both ends of the "on the money" square stock, then draw a few concentric circles to help you keep track. Keep all eight sides approximately the same distance from the circles while beveling and tapering.

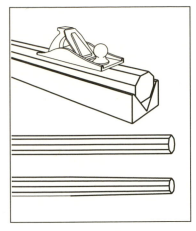

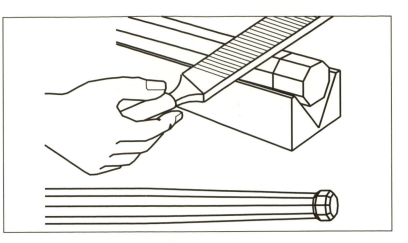

It is helpful to knock together a cradle from scrap wood. Orient the grain toward the top of the flagpole and plane with that direction. Keep rotating the pole so the cuts are even as the four beveled sides form an octagon.

Taper the upper quarter of the staff toward the head. Begin close to the tapered end and shave a little from each of the sides, starting back a bit farther with each pass. To preserve the knob for shaping, stop planing the taper when you have reduced the staff diameter by about a quarter. Continue tapering the top of the pole below the knob with a rasp, file, and sanding block. Bevel facets into the top of the knob with a bench sander, rasp, or fine-toothed backsaw. Cut matching bevels below the knob, making it spherical or oval. Increase the pole taper just below the knob with rasp and file, matching the facets in the knob.

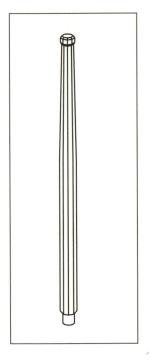

File a tenon at the base to match the diameter and depth of the socket it will go in. Sand the staff the first time with a block to maintain the flats of the eight facets; sand it again with light sandpaper to smooth the ridges between facets. If you used teak, apply a little teak oil and you're done. Protect all other woods with several coats of varnish.

ROD RACKS

J-hook racks mounted high in a forepeak or inside a cockpit locker provide out-of-the-way but handy stowage for fishing rods. You can fashion similar racks for other long items such as boat hooks, pole spears, and awning poles.

MATERIALS:

Hardwood, plugs, mounting fasteners

TOOLS:

Saw, drill, spade bits, rasp, sander

Lay out the hook on 1-by stock and drill the center hole with an appropriate spade bit. Use a sabersaw to cut the rack out and to open the J. For a single rod, fashion a pair of wooden hooks (or a single hook) for the rod, and a hoop bracket for the handle.

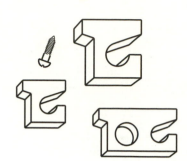

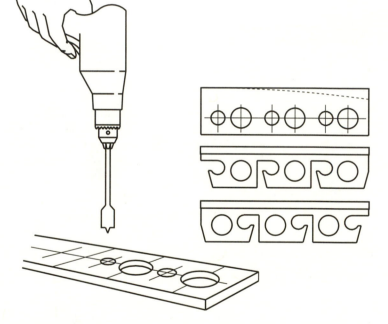

Multiple rods take less space when they are racked heel-to-toe, so alternate holes and J-hooks in a multirod bracket. Attach the racks to a perpendicular base such as an exposed deck beam and fasten them to a horizontal surface with screws through the bracket. If the brackets are thin, fasten them through an attached T-base.

CUTTING BOARD

Every galley needs a cutting board for filleting the day's catch and cutting limes for the evening's gin and tonic. One that's designed to fit over the sink adds counter space rather than occupying it—an added benefit in a cramped galley.

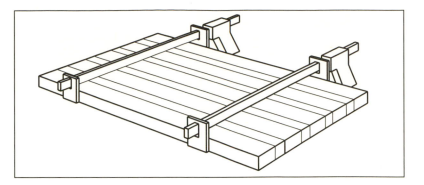

MATERIALS:

Maple (preferred) or ash, perhaps a contrasting dark wood, epoxy

TOOLS:

Saw, clamps, drill, hole saw, router, palm sander

You can fashion a small cutting board from solid wood, but if the board is going to be large enough to cover the sink you'll want to laminate it. Laminating provides needed width and exposes edge grain, which is generally tighter. Also, a laminated board has less tendency to warp.

Cover your work surface with waxed paper and butt glue the strips together with epoxy. The miniwork platform (page 51) allows you to apply clamping pressure with matched pairs of wedges driven against each other, or use bar clamps if you have them.

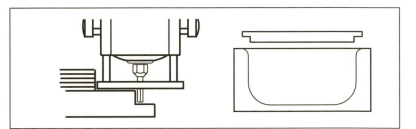

After the glue cures, saw your cutting board from the laminated blank $3/8$ to $1/2$ inch ($3/4$ to 1 inch overall) larger than the sink well. Round the corners and sand the edges to give the router's edge guide a smooth riding surface. Rout a rabbet around the perimeter of the bottom to create an island that fits inside the sink and holds the board in place.

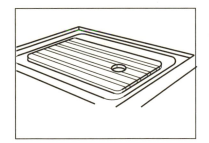

One shortcut you might consider is buying a ready-made cutting or bread board and cut and rabbet it to fit your sink. For a single-sink galley, consider making the board shorter than the sink—you'll get a cutting surface and access to the sink at the same time.

JOINERY

Instead of carving a single item from solid or laminated block, let's fashion two or more such pieces and put them together into an assembly. This is called joinery, and it differs from what we have already done only in its requirement for strong and attractive joints between the pieces.

SOME BETTER JOINTS TO FREQUENT

Butt joints are just like they sound: two pieces are butted together and fastened. A butt-joined corner (also called a case joint) that is glued *and* screwed will be strong enough for small products. Clean, square ends are essential.

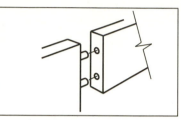

Dowel joints are butt joints that are reinforced with wooden dowels. They will support more weight and hold up better anywhere crewmembers might lurch by your handiwork with armloads of heavy gear.

Miter joints are diagonal butt joints. Their main advantage is that they hide all end grain, but they are weak unless reinforced.

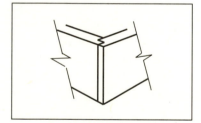

Rabbet joints are stronger than butt joints because of the additional glue surface. They are particularly easy to cut with a router.

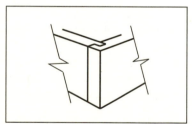

Dado slot joints are similar to rabbet joints except they are used to join one board inside the edge of another that has been rabbetted. A wider dado slot well in from the ends is shown on page 114.

Lap joints, because they greatly increase gluing area, are much stronger than butt and miter joints. Various types of lap joints have specific uses and advantages. For example, joining rails and stiles with a corner half-lap creates a very rigid door frame.

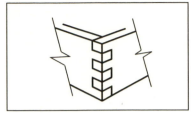

Finger joints, also called box joints, look complicated but are quick to cut with a table saw. If you're working with thin stock you can hand-cut finger joints with a sabersaw or handsaw and finish them off with a file. Slot depth equals the thickness of the material. Work out equal tab width and spacing to net a full tab at opposing edges. Finger joints are best mastered on scrap before cutting premium lumber. Well-fitted finger joints provide admirable strength.

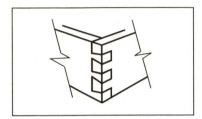

Dovetail joints are the hallmarks of craftsmanship, but hand-cut dovetail joints take a bit more time, care, and dedication than most weekend woodworkers possess. Commercial jigs are available that, when used with a router, allow you to cut perfect dovetail joints almost as easily as rabbet joints.

CUTTING CORNERS

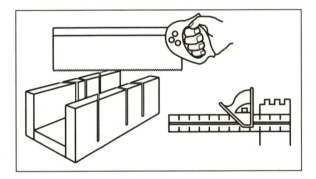

A miter box is handy for cutting straight butt joints and mitered corners, and the same backsaw (or any fine-toothed saw) can cut a finger joint by carefully sawing into the end along the marked-off lines to a depth equal to its thickness. Saw a couple of diagonal cuts into the corners and finish off with a file.

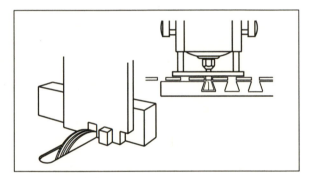

Power tools can be put to good use cutting various corner joints. Cut finger joints on a table saw with the help of a block of wood with two slots at the desired spacing. A tab that fits the just-cut slot positions the piece for the next cut.

A router, in addition to cutting rabbets, dadoes, and rounded edges, can cut dovetails with the help of a spacing jig. A sabersaw (not shown) can produce straight cuts with the help of fences and guides.

SEASONINGS BOX

Any open-top box is handy for containing small items. This one keeps spice jars close to the cook.

MATERIALS:

Thin wood, glue

TOOLS:

Sabersaw, router, finishing sander

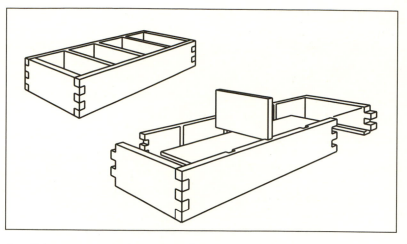

Cut all the components from thin wood ($^3/_8$ to $^1/_2$ inch in thickness). Vertical slots in the box sides let you insert dividers to keep containers upright.

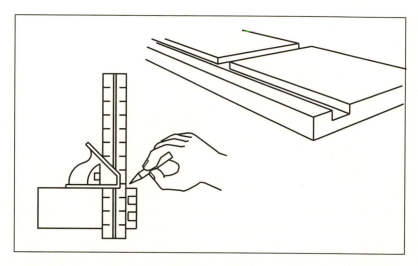

Finger joints are optional, but make sure that the corner joint you choose is strong. Cut the bottom wider and longer to fit into slots dadoed near the bottom edge. Use a router and straight-edge to cut the shallow dado slots.

DRINK HOLDERS

Cans that are wedged into a corner of the cockpit and glasses that are set against a toerail inevitably get knocked over. A drink tray that fits over a binnacle guard, around a mizzen mast, or onto a stanchion avoids these messy spills.

MATERIALS:

Wood, plugs, screws, glue

TOOLS:

Sabersaw, drill, hole saw, router, finishing sander

A grab bar forward of the binnacle is a potential mounting location. If the sides of the bar cant outward toward the bottom, a slot in the drink tray makes an adequate mount. A grab bar with vertical legs will need stops for a slotted tray, or you can split the tray and bolt the halves together to clamp it to the bar.

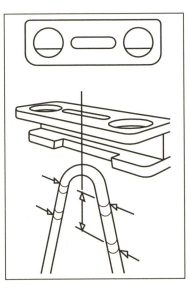

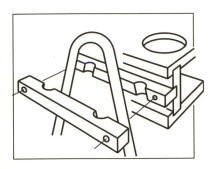

To make wooden clamps for a round bar, use a spade bit to drill a hole (or holes) the same diameter as the tubing, then saw the piece in half through the center of the hole(s). Be sure to cut the wood apart with the grain so the grain runs perpendicular to the clamping fasteners. The saw-blade kerf will reduce the clamp's diameter enough to grip the bar when installed. With the bar in the center, fasten the two halves back together with wood screws, or bolt the halves together if you will someday want to remove the clamp.

A mast that's located in a cockpit makes an excellent tray pedestal at anchor, but a mast-mounted drink holder can be a nuisance under sail. If, however, you design the drink holder with a clamp that lets you install and remove it easily, you can take advantage of the mizzenmast when the cocktail flag is hoisted and still sail without banging body parts against your creation.

Slotted lugs that extend from the holder and flank the mast can be removed quickly while underway. A more permanent collar around the mast, fitted with a slot in which to insert a metal tab fastened to the tray, can provide a quick-lift removal.

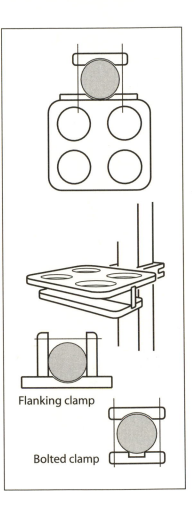

Flanking clamp

Bolted clamp

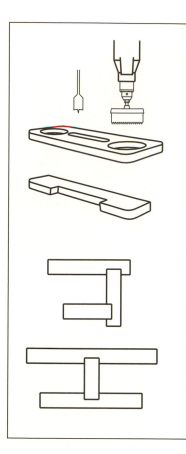

Drink holders generally consist of three components: a top piece with holes to accommodate drink containers, a shelf below to support the containers, and a vertical spacer that connects the two. The mounting bracket can be an integral feature of either of the horizontal pieces, or it can be attached to the vertical piece. Cockpit racks need to be sturdy to withstand the inevitable knocks and bumps they'll receive.

The amount of space that's between the top and bottom of a holder depends on the height of the containers you want the rack to hold; the size of the holes depends on the diameter of the glasses, cups, or cans. (Don't forget to allow space for insulating sleeves.) Holders that will receive cups need handle slots. The number of holes likely will be limited by the space you are willing to allot.

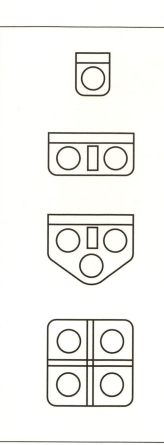

BINOCULAR RACK

A dedicated rack or box provides a secure spot for binoculars when not in use. You might want one in the cabin and one in the cockpit.

MATERIALS:

Wood, plugs, screws, glue

TOOLS:

Sabersaw, drill, router, finishing sander

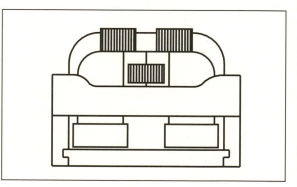

You can build an enclosed box for your binoculars or, if you prefer, fabricate an open rack with a rail to secure them.

The inside dimensions of the rack are dictated by the size of the binoculars. Because binoculars should always be "at the ready," the rack needs easy access. The front rail (or panel) should be above center but low enough to grab the binoculars easily. A snug fit prevents the binoculars from banging around inside the rack.

In this design, the bottom is dadoed for a slotted joint along the sides, and the rail is let in flush to front.

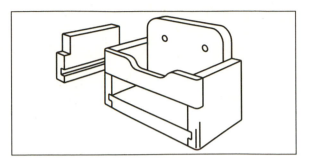

WINCH HANDLE BOX

Winch handles can't be left in top-action winches, but they need to be within easy reach. A finely crafted wooden box mounted near winches can be a more attractive handle repository than commercial plastic holders.

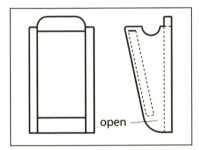

open

Using 3/4-inch stock helps withstand bumps and allows you to assemble the sides to the back and face with butt joints. Fasten with 1 1/4-inch #8 screws and epoxy, plugging the holes. Design the height and angle to support the handle at the bottom with the grip in one of the top notches.

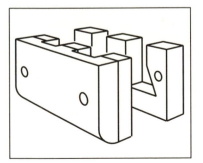

Angle the bottom and round the corners and edges so the box will shed lines rather than snag them. Give the box a generous drain hole or omit the bottom entirely, as shown here.

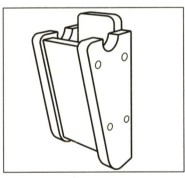

An alternative to a winch handle box is a rack configured to the working end of the handle. When installed hard against the cockpit wall, this laminated block contains cutouts to hold a pair of fairly flat winch handles, spanners, or roller reef handles. This rack could be designed with an additional stand-off block to clear cockpit seat lids (see illustration on page 14).

MATERIALS:

Wood, plugs, screws, glue

TOOLS:

Sabersaw, drill, router, finishing sander

Most boatowners can make good use of a few additional shelves inside lockers, on bulkheads, or against the hull sides. Plywood is particularly suitable for long, wide shelves, but it is also a good choice for smaller shelves. The odd angles and radii of a boat's interior often require some careful measuring and scribing for a snug fit.

ADDING A SHELF

MATERIALS:

Plywood, ³⁄₄-inch square stock, screws

TOOLS:

Saw, drill

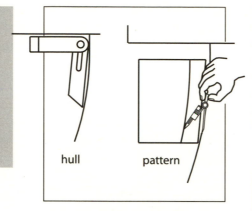

hull   pattern

To fit a shelf against the curvature of the hull, first cut a pattern from scrap wood or cardboard. Hold the pattern in position against the hull and strike a parallel curve using a pencil compass. Cut this curve on your pattern, then trace it onto the shelf.

Hidden cleats can be a bit utilitarian. A straight bevel should be adequate to set cleats square to the shelf. Screw cleats to wooden members; attach them to the inside of the hull with polyurethane adhesive.

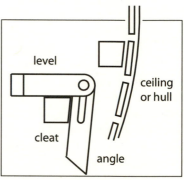

level

ceiling or hull

cleat

angle

fasten cleat to side and shelf to cleat

Fasten larger shelves to side cleats with wood screws from below. A longitudinal cleat will prevent the shelf from sagging with or without fastenings. For self-contained hanging shelves, a longitudinal cleat is the only means of fastening, so cut it wide enough for clearance to attach the shelf from below if possible. Otherwise, screw and plug the shelf from above.

BRACKETED SHELVES

Add a bracketed shelf (brackets above, below, or both) to hold equipment, books, and goodies.

MATERIALS:

Hardwood ply-wood, veneer tape, screws

TOOLS:

Saw, router, fin-ishing sander, drill

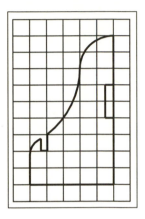

If you see a rack that might look good on your boat, draft its contour on grid paper. Enlarge the grid to the desired size and connect the dots to net a full-size pattern.

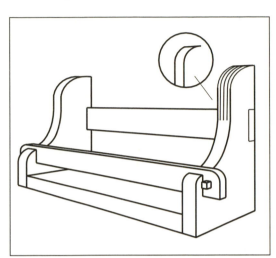

Use a sabersaw and a plywood blade to cut nice arcs and curves into the plywood brackets. The curved edges of the plywood will be concealed with veneer tape, and the straight edges with molding or tape.

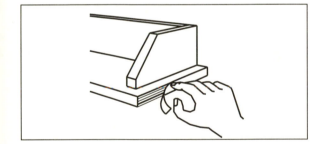

Using veneer edge tape that matches the wood is a quick and easy way to conceal plywood edges. Iron-on edge tape comes with hot-glue backing and is the easiest to apply. Otherwise, use contact cement or carpenter's glue to adhere the veneer to the edges. Carefully trim the installed tape with a mat knife and, with a light touch, sand the cut edges flush with the faces of the plywood.

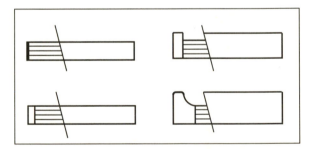

Wood is a bit more durable than veneer, especially along an exposed edge. If you choose to finish the edges with wood, use thin strips that either match or contrast with the plywood. Trim that is wider than the plywood will stiffen it and can double as a fiddle rail. Edge trim can be plain rectangular stock or fancy molding. You can buy a variety of suitable molding from your chandler or lumber yard, or you can mill your own with a router.

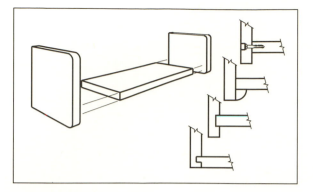

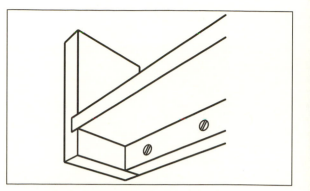

How you join the various shelf components will depend on whether the shelf will serve light or heavy duty and whether it will be protected or subjected to inadvertent abuse. Design accordingly.

For bracketed shelves without a back, it helps to extend the ends below the shelf to provide space for an attachment cleat. If you use plywood, take the time to seal the backsides of the brackets and shelves to reduce the amount of moisture the plywood might absorb.

If you need to capture your onboard books in a self-contained rack nestled in a tight space, a notched rail (an alternative to the pegged version shown earlier) allows easy access.

BOXED SHELF

It's a rare boat that can't make use of an open boxed shelf, or one with sliding doors, or one with drawers to hold tapes, spare parts, or navigation tools.

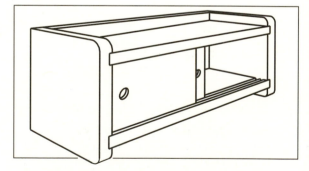

MATERIALS:

Hardwood plywood, veneer tape, screws

TOOLS:

Saw, router, finishing sander, drill

The boxed shelf shown here is a bracketed shelf with an enclosed top and back. This is a small addition, but a similar design of a larger scale could become a case enclosed by a hinged door outfitted with drawers.

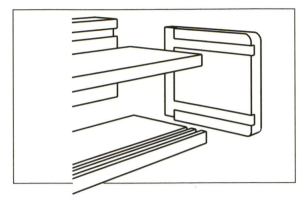

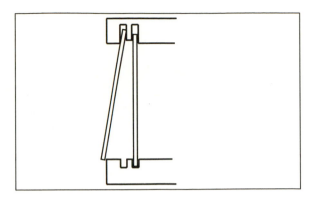

Rout dadoes into the sides for the top and bottom and a rabbet for the back. Cut tracks into the top and bottom for thin plywood or dark Plexiglass doors. Thin ply that's sold as door skins can be veneered with your species of choice. Veneering is just a matter of gluing wood to wood, a task that's well within the ability of the weekend woodworker.

The trick, if there is one, is to cut the doors so they overlap in length when installed, clear the lower rail for installation, and are tall enough to be captured in the tracks when vertically in place. Dado the upper tracks deeper than the bottom tracks so you can slip the doors up and into the upper tracks when they're ready to install. A slight bevel or undercut of the top tracks will give you the needed clearance.

ELECTRONICS RACK

When shopping for a new CD player for the boat, you might not find a thin profile design that fits nicely into a bulkhead rack. Most will remind you of a Ford Taurus. Ovals are big, molded cases are "in," and a customized rack will be required.

MATERIALS:

Hardwood plywood, veneer tape, screws

TOOLS:

Saw, router, finishing sander, drill

When building a rack for a portable electronic component, first take a close look at the product. Its case should be the rack's inside dimensions—but a closer look might reveal some appendages that need to fit inside the rack. And, being portable means the item must be lifted out for recharging. Handles and knobs can fit into slots and cutouts and might eliminate the need for a rail.

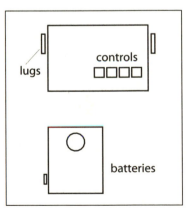

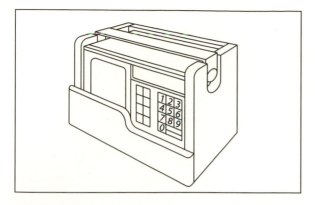

Omit rails and make cutouts in the sides to afford access to buttons or to view display screens.

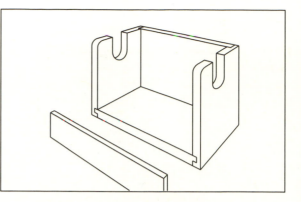

Select material thickness to complement the lines of the component and to ensure that the rack is substantial enough to protect the equipment.

FLUSH-MOUNTED ELECTRONICS

Less portable electronics or a new power panel can be flush mounted in an existing cabinet or bulkhead. Select a location with good visibility and easy access. The backside should also be accessible for wiring and troubleshooting.

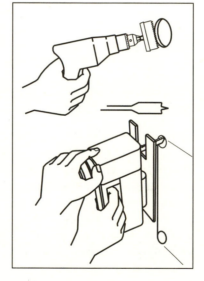

A flush-mounted component typically has a flange that overlaps the mounting hole. Determine the opening size from the installation instructions and make the cutout with a hole saw or sabersaw as appropriate.

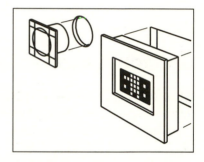

A boxed frame will finish an installation in an adjacent space.

Capture with molding attached to box and bulkhead at the backside.

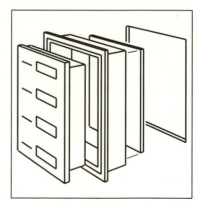

To recess a power panel and enclose the backside, use a boxed frame. Build the frame deep enough to house the panel and wiring and capture the box in the hole with molding on both sides. Give mitered corners some trim molding and remember that a removable back panel gives you access for troubleshooting.

FLAG RACK

A bona fide signal-flag rack has 40 spaces—26 for the alphabet, 10 for the numerals, one for the code/answer pennant, and three for repeaters. It may also have a drawer or locker to hold the national flag or ensign. If your boat doesn't have space for such an elaborate rack, perhaps you can find a spot that will house a small rack in which you can stow the flags you use the most.

Decide on the number and size of the compartments to fit the space.

MATERIALS:

Hardwood plywood, veneer tape, carpenter's glue

TOOLS:

Saw, router, finishing sander

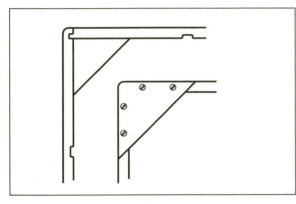

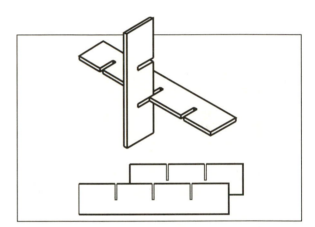

Decide how you will construct the corners, then look at different ways to attach the grid—square cleats, quarter-round molding, or let into the frame.

A full back is recommended if the rack will be installed on anything other than a flat bulkhead or cabinet side. (A back also serves to keep the shell rigid.) Corner joints should be strong—slotted dadoes are good because the edges can be nicely rounded over. For a backless rack, a corner gusset let in flush will keep the assembly square. Grid components should be longer than the opening (by about one-third the thickness of the materials used) to let into dado slots routed into the inside faces.

Cut the pieces for the grid and slot them slightly more than half the width of the board at every point of intersection. Fit the vertical and horizontal pieces together at the notches.

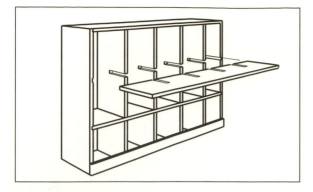

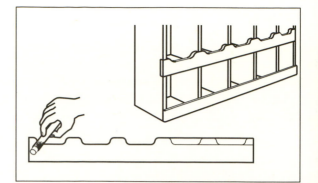

Using your carpenter's square, first glue and assemble the frame corners, then glue and screw in place the back or corner gussets. Finally, glue the grid ends into the receiving slots.

A fiddle rail can run straight across or dip at every compartment (or at each divider)—just make sure that the rail is tall enough to keep the flag in its bin. Wrap some sandpaper around a dowel to help you sand the contoured cutouts. Veneer tape all exposed plywood edges. Fiddle rails could be cut from solid wood.

MEDICINE CABINET

Build a box, install some shelves, hinge a framed mirror on the front—and you have a medicine cabinet.

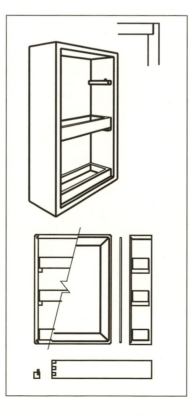

MATERIALS:

Wood, plywood, veneer tape, mirror. epoxy

TOOLS:

Saw, router, finishing sander, drill

The shell should be a little more substantial than the one described for a flag rack, but the joinery is similar, with one exception: use $1/2$- to $3/4$-inch lumber or hardwood plywood. Size to fit the space available.

A small, removable open box (similar to the spice box) can rest on pegged cleats. Compartmentalizing one or more of the boxes will help keep the Band-Aids away from the Dramamine.

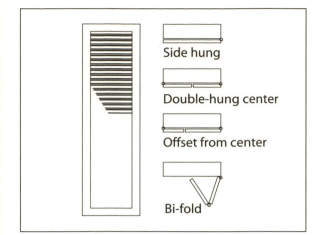

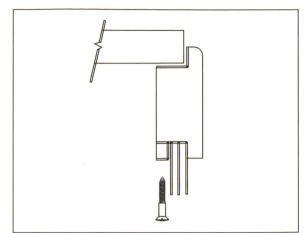

Even with bulkhead space, clearance for the door(s) will guide your overall size and door arrangement. Options include single, double-hung, offset, or bifold doors. A continuous (piano) hinge is suggested, especially if you add a mirror to the door.

The door frame should be cut from stock that's thick enough to rabbet in a ledge to capture the mirror, the mirror's thickness, and a backing sheet of thick plywood to protect the silvered back. All these items should be captured by a band of molding inset flush with the thickness of the door frame. Glue and tack the molding in place with small brads or small round-headed screws.

HALF-HULL MODEL

Making a half-hull model is something of a departure from the other projects in this book, but if you are game, here's how to do it.

MATERIALS:

Thin hardwood, carpenter's glue

TOOLS:

Saw, finishing sander, plan drawings

Years ago, boat designers carved full- or half-hull models as their first step in hull design. Once the hull form was to their liking, they sliced the model apart and picked off the lines. Half-hull modeling reverses this process.

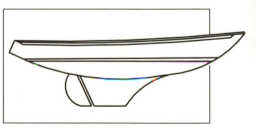

The plans for your boat have three views. You are interested in the shape of the waterlines viewed from above and the station lines viewed from the ends. Waterlines are recorded as plus (+) and minus (-) above and below the design waterline—also known as the lift.

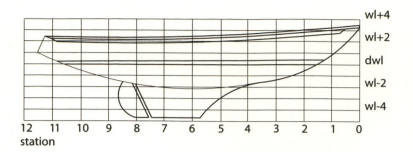

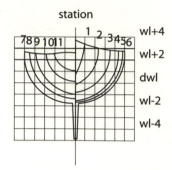

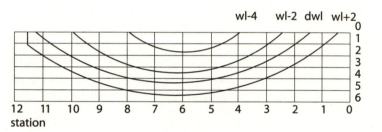

The best way to approach scaling is to work to available milled wood thickness. If the drawing shows waterlines spaced $1/16$ inch apart, and the overall length of the drawing is 6 inches, these dimensions will rise proportionally when enlarged. So if you use $1/8$-inch material, your finished half-model will be 12 inches. After you decide on the scale you want, take the drawings to a photocopy shop for enlarging or reducing to a working size. Get two or three sets reproduced to scale. Paste copies of the plan view to the stock.

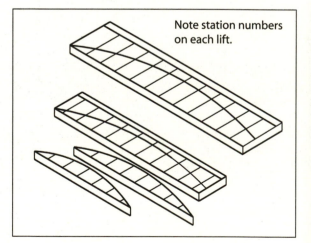

Note station numbers on each lift.

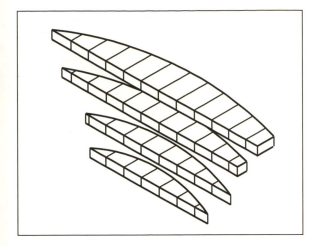

Cut out the half-hull waterline for each lift. You are working from the widest waterline in, so the stock will be sufficiently wide to carve fair lines. Mark the station locations on the flat side of the lifts (the boat's centerline).

Remove paper pattern and glue up the blank. You will be pleasantly surprised how these lines that are cut into the thin stock conform to the drawn lines.

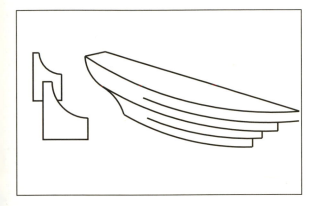

Use copies of the end views to cut profiles of the hull shape at each station. Use these templates to test the shape of the model at each station as the carving progresses.

Carve back to the boat's lines using flat and round rasps and files. You might have to do some carving with a chisel to get close to the lines. Continue with flat and rounded rasps, and then use coarse sandpaper (80- to 100-grit) down to the lines in the cut lifts. Finish shaping and fairing with progressively finer grades of sandpaper.

Look at the decorative plaques described in Chapter 2. One of those shapes might provide a complementary base for your completed half-hull model.

INDEX

International Marine/
Ragged Mountain Press

A Division of The McGraw-Hill Companies

10 9 8 7 6 5 4 3 2 1

Copyright © 1998 International Marine, a division of The McGraw-Hill Companies.

Library of Congress Cataloging-in-Publication Data
Graves, Garth.
  Boatowner's weekend woodworking / Garth Graves.
        p.   cm.—(International Marine sailboat library)
    Includes index.
    ISBN 0-07-024696-3 (hc.)
    1. Wooden boats—Maintenance and repair. 2. Woodwork I. Title.
    II. Series.
  VM322.G73 1998
  623.8'44—dc21   98-19876
                                            CIP

Questions regarding the content of this book should be addressed to:
  International Marine
  P.O. Box 220
  Camden, ME 04843
  www.internationalmarine.com

Questions regarding the ordering of this book should be addressed to:
  The McGraw-Hill Companies
  Customer Service Department
  P.O. Box 547
  Blacklick, OH 43004
  Retail customers: 1-800-262-4729
  Bookstores: 1-800-722-4726
  www.books.mcgraw-hill.com

This book is printed on 60-pound Renew Opaque Vellum, an acid-free paper that contains 50 percent recycled waste paper (preconsumer) and 10 percent postconsumer waste paper. ♲

Illustrations on pages 2–3, 8–9, 22, 32, 34–35, 66–67, 68, 80–81, and 104–105 and back cover by
  Jim Sollers. All other art by Garth Graves.
Printed by R.R. Donnelly, Crawfordsville, IN
Design and layout by Ann Aspell
Production by Janet Robbins
Production assistance by Shannon Thomas; Mary Ann Hensel
Edited by Jonathan Eaton; Nancy Hauswald; Tom McCarthy
Cover photo by William Thuss, Thuss Photography

GARTH GRAVES has been a woodworker for over 40 years. He's spent more than 25 of those years designing and building projects for boats, including his own 27-foot wooden sloop, *Sea-Fever,* and has contributed time to building a well-known tall ship, the replica revenue cutter *California.* He is the author of *Yacht Craftsman's Handbook: 50 Woodworking Projects* and has written articles for *Fine Woodworking, WoodenBoat, Popular Mechanics,* and *Better Homes & Gardens.*

THE INTERNATIONAL MARINE SAILBOAT LIBRARY

Boatowner's Weekend Woodworking has company:

100 Fast and Easy Boat Improvements
by Don Casey
Hardcover, 144 pages, 285 illustrations, $21.95. Item No. 013402-2

Sailboat Refinishing
by Don Casey
Hardcover, 144 pages, 350 illustrations, $21.95. Item No. 013225-9

Sailboat Hull & Deck Repair
by Don Casey
Hardcover, 144 pages, 350 illustrations, $21.95. Item No. 013369-7

Canvaswork & Sail Repair
by Don Casey
Hardcover, 144 pages, 350 illustrations, $21.95. Item No. 013391-3

The Sailor's Assistant:
Reference Data for Maintenance, Repair, & Cruising
by John Vigor
Hardcover, 176 pages, 140 illustrations, $21.95. Item No. 067476-0

Troubleshooting Marine Diesels
by Peter Compton
Hardcover, 176 pages, 200 illustrations, $21.95. Item No. 012354-3

Inspecting the Aging Sailboat
by Don Casey
Hardcover, 144 pages, 300 illustrations, $21.95. Item No. 013394-8